MAPPING THE ROAD TO YOUR DESTINY

My Long Road from Costa Rica to Oklahoma and Beyond

by

Rodolfo (Rudy) Blanco

with Karen Hardin

TABLE OF

CONTENTS

INTRODUCTION

In my company, Pathway Services Inc., cities, states and even other countries hire us to take inventory of every single road in their jurisdiction, take pictures, and sensor data to analyze its state and provide a report of the condition and what needs to be done to preserve or restore them. In essence we are mapping out the entire region of these areas for successful paths for the present and future. What if we could do that with people?

If I could do one thing with my life, it would be to help others take inventory of their roads in life, analyze them, understand them, and discover from them their destiny and the joy that comes in finding that destiny. We each are on a journey. We each have a destiny and when we find it, we find true fulfillment and joy. That is why I have written this book.

The reason I have chosen to share my story is for all the other "Rudy's" out there. You have a dream, a desire to do something with your life. But you have no idea what that means. In your heart you are asking the same questions I was asking, "Why am I here? What is my purpose? Is there really a God? And if there is, does He care about me?"

I can tell you there is and He does.

My story is for anyone who desires to make a difference with their life, but is not sure the path to get there. In our own ability we cannot. Yet we each have a destiny to fulfill—our hearts beat for it. Until the hardships and disappointments in life come to snuff it out, we all have a deep desire to make a difference. I want to tell you that you can, and that desire comes from God.

I'm just a regular guy, born into a poor family from a poor country. Yet, today I am the owner of a successful business with branches in both the United States and Costa Rica. The dream birthed in my heart when I was a young man, still in my twenties has come to pass, not because of who I am, but because of my Creator. I am blessed beyond measure and more importantly, God has used me to be a blessing to others in ways I had never dreamed. My story, in fact, completely changed when I simply made the decision to give Him a chance to prove Himself to me.

As you read these pages, I want to challenge you to give Him the chance to prove Himself to you. Because if you will, He will.

Part I

FROM COSTA RICA TO OKLAHOMA

Chapter 1

THE CHALLENGE

"Please do something with me, God. I know you can!" I pleaded with a God I didn't even know. But He knew me.

I believed there was a God out there somewhere, and I believed He could do something with my life. I desperately wanted Him to do something with my life. I believe we all have that deep desire ingrained within us. We want our lives to count--to matter in the bigger scheme of things. That desire comes from God and each of us has within us a seed for greatness--a gift, talent or ability that God created within us and wants to use. That journey of discovery is called life. It is up to us what we choose to do with it.

The desire to do something with my life burned within me. It was calling me, compelling me. The only problem was I did not know what I was supposed to do. I didn't know exactly what gifts I possessed or what to do with what I had. So, I decided it couldn't hurt to see what God could do. I decided to make him an offer.

"God, I will give you ten years to do something with my life."

At that time, I was twenty-nine years old and really wanted my own business. I decided that if He was really God, then my pact to give him ten years should give Him plenty of time to accomplish that plan if He was real! That crazy prayer was just the start of an amazing ride. When we give God the green light to work in our lives, He will always take that opportunity to show up and show off. He's just waiting for that invitation. Little did I know what I was getting myself into with a prayer that gave God the reins.

What happened over the next ten years probably shouldn't have happened considering the background from which I came. I was just a poor kid, raised in a poor country, and in all likelihood, I should have stayed poor.

I grew up in Cartago, Costa Rica in the foothills of an active volcano. Our home was in a neighborhood known as the INVU which was a government housing development for poor families. My parents, six siblings, an uncle and I shared a tiny four-bedroom home. Since I was the youngest of the boys, I was usually the "floater," the one looking for a bed or somewhere to sleep at night since the "boys" room had only three beds for four boys. Our house just wasn't large enough to accommodate us all. Our electricity was often shut off because money was always tight, and my dad couldn't pay the utility bill. It was a day to celebrate when Dad got his paycheck. That usually meant that the lights would get turned back on and we would "feast" for several days. That is, until the money ran out again. Then, for the most part, our diet usually consisted of rice and beans, beans and rice…and "gallo pinto" which is simply left-over rice and beans!

"Rodolfo," my dad would call. "Go knock on the neighbor's door and see if he can lend us a few bucks," Dad would instruct. This wasn't uncommon and I was always a little embarrassed as I knocked on his door. Don (which means Sir in Spanish) Oscar was a gracious man and usually responded with a small bill into my outstretched hand. That money helped keep food on our table or provided for other necessities. The odd thing is, I don't ever remember Dad asking me to return any of the money we borrowed!

Although we didn't have much in the way of material possessions, we were a close-knit family. During summer break and after school, my siblings and I could often be found in the fields surrounding our neighborhood which became our play yard. Many happy hours were spent exploring and playing soccer or "Cowboys and Indians" with the other neighborhood kids as we sucked the sweetness from a stick of sugar cane we had discovered or oranges from the neighbor's orange tree which we sneaked when we could much to their chagrin. Life was simple, but it was happy. Yet even from an early age, the draw toward what would eventually be my vocation began to emerge.

I believe the gift that is within us calls to us. I think there is no better example of this than high-wire artist Philippe Petit. At a young age he snuck under the canvas of a circus tent to watch the performances. It was the first time he had ever seen a circus and he became mesmerized by the high-wire walkers. Afterwards, he went home and strung rope between two trees and dedicated hours each day to learning how to walk that rope. It wasn't just a childhood dream or infatuation. It was a call that stayed with him. He was consumed with learning to be a wire walker because I believe the gift within him called to him. Not many people have the ability, balance and stamina to be a wire walker. How did he know he could even do it? But inside something drew him to it. And when he acted on it, the gift and his understanding of his gift began to grow. The seed that also began to grow was the idea that he could use that gift to make a difference with his life, and he did. In 1974, Philippe came to the United States and did the unthinkable when he strung a wire between the two towers of the World Trade Center and walked across suspended hundreds of feet in the air with no safety line attached. He did what no one else had ever done because he pursued that call within him.

What is that call within you? What do you find you are good at? What continues to call you to it? And are you willing to dedicate your life to do

11

it? The answer to those questions is where we make a difference. For each of us can make a difference in life when we recognize our gift, pursue and develop that gift and let God use our gift.

I found I was good at taking things apart and putting things together and discovering how they worked. I was always a curious kind of kid and loved to learn. My father was a mechanic who worked for the government, servicing their heavy equipment vehicles such as bulldozers and dump trucks. That was his gift and he kept those vehicles in top notch condition. Eventually when he had saved enough to buy a vehicle for our family, he was the one that did the repairs. I remember the time that the engine quit and had to be overhauled. Of course, Dad did it and right in our front yard. I was his helper. As he took the engine apart, I was under the car with him asking questions about every piece he unhooked and put into my hand as he dismantled that engine. I soaked in the knowledge as I watched him work, intrigued at the process. Those times watching him and working with him were an education that would serve me well years later.

Since I loved learning how things worked, I guess it was natural that I also loved science. That can be a dangerous combination! One time I discovered a discarded headlight my Dad had left in our front yard. My mind immediately began to whirl with possibilities. I picked it up and walked over to a live electrical outlet. I wondered what would happen if I touched the metal end of the bulb directly to the 120v outlet. At ten or eleven years of age, this made sense in my mind and I figured it should work as the electricity was on the outlet and the light worked with electricity. So, I held the glass bulb tight as I made the metal end connect to the outlet. A shower of sparks erupted, spraying across my hand and in all directions. I dropped the bulb in surprise. Fortunately, I wasn't electrocuted since I wasn't directly touching the metal conduit. However, that little incident didn't deter my insatiable need for knowledge in the least. If anything, it only stirred me further. I was never afraid to try new things or reach for the unknown.

Money was always an issue in our home, or the lack of it I should say. We just never had much. Dad worked hard to provide, but there were a lot of mouths to feed. Extra money for candy, treats or extracurricular activities just wasn't available, so I decided to find a job---as an altar boy.

Although I wouldn't call us "religious," my family attended mass at the Catholic Church. I learned the altar boys were paid ten cents for each mass in which they served. That may not sound like much now, but it was huge for me and well worth the time investment. So, I served at as many masses as I could every Sunday to get paid. But even that action was God's guiding hand in my life in small ways long before I knew Him personally. God has ways of leading us to the places and people we need, to speak to us and guide us in the destiny He has for us. It was there in those services that I was exposed over and over again to the Gospel. The rituals of Mass held no meaning for me really, but in each service the priest would read two passages from the letters of the apostles followed by one passage from one of the four Gospels in the New Testament. This was my favorite part of the services and I listened intently, my spirit hungry for Truth. On some weekends, I would sit through as many as ten masses. So, while I was getting paid, I was also learning more about God.

At that time, my picture of God was that of an old man sitting on a big chair up in the sky, ready to punish me for the slightest mistake. Yet there in mass, as I heard the priest read the scriptures, there was life. Although I didn't understand it all, it drew me to God and questions often rolled over in my mind. I think they are questions common to all of us. Maybe you have asked those same questions. Where do I come from? Why am I here? Is heaven real? What happens when I die? Is there really a God and if there is, why can't I see Him? Does He really care about me? Does my life really matter?

These questions concerned me, and there didn't seem to be any immediate answers.

Chapter 2

A Drastic Change

There are moments in all of our lives that are defining moments. Others are complete game-changers. Transitions in life are game changers based on the choices we make. At those times in life we face a fork in the road. We have to make a choice on which path we will choose and the road we choose will set the course for our lives. It's important that we choose wisely. But even in these decisions, I can look back and recognize how God was guiding me even then.

One such game-changing moment happened when I was just thirteen. My father passed away at the age of sixty-two with complications from arthritis and rheumatism. Although he had been sick for a while, and we all knew his health was declining, it still came as a shock. It changed me. It changed us all. My older brother, Carlos, had to step into the role of primary breadwinner alongside my Mom. It was hard to come to grips with the fact that my dad was never going to be there again.

Childhood changed in that moment and we all had to grow up quickly. Although we had been poor before, now we all had to pull together to survive. As I look back over that time I realize that although it was a time of grief for the loss of my father, my family and I actually bonded together tighter than before. But something else changed in me that year which I can't really explain. Although there were many hard changes that year, the fact that it drew my family even closer one was for the better.

Up to that point I had been just an average student with average grades. I wasn't great in school and didn't really enjoy studying. After my dad was gone that changed, maybe because I realized the necessity of doing well in school to get a good job. It was as if the light bulb suddenly turned on. Things began to make sense in class. Things began to just "click." Instead of ranking in the middle of the class with my grade point average, I was now in the top two or three students! I was not only making great grades, but I now had an appetite for learning and knowledge. I loved the entire process. It was a change that paved the way to my future.

Now at the head of my class, several times my teachers wanted to put me in a study group with my classmates for various projects or to study for a test. I never liked the study groups. For me, studying was serious business and I found the study groups for most students were more about fun and games. Because of that, I usually pulled away by myself to study for the tests to make sure I was prepared. After I knew I was ready, I would join the group to "study" with them.

Studying and learning became my passion. Once I graduated from high school it also opened another door for me. I graduated high school and was accepted to the Instituto Tecnológico de Costa Rica. It was a relatively new school back then, but has since grown to be well-known for its high standards and draws the top students from all over Central America. Some have referred to it as the M.I.T. of Central America.

The fact that I was even in college, coming from my family background, was no small accomplishment. I was studying industrial production engineering. Like my father, I had a way with putting things together and seeing how things fit. While I enjoyed my classes, like any other college kid, I also enjoyed just having fun. In that season that often included hanging out at the local "discoteca."

It was in my last year of college as my buddy, Jorge Tencio and I went to hang out at the disco that I encountered another game-changer in my life. It could have been seen as simply a chance encounter, but it was an incident that would forever change my life.

Unlikely encounters can happen almost anywhere during our lives. However, chance encounters aren't always just because of chance. I have learned that God has a design and destiny for our lives. Even when I didn't know Him, I hungered for Him. Even then He was guiding my steps to the right places and the right people.

One evening in 1976, Jorge had invited me to go with him to one of our favorite discotecas in Cartago. Our "fun" usually involved a few drinks and dancing to "cumbia," "salsa," and "boleros" music. We danced primarily because it meant we could meet girls.

We walked in and sat at our usual booth. The disco was popular and it was an inexpensive activity. My brothers, friends and I would spend hours there talking, eating and just spending time together. Once seated, I scanned the dimly lit room to see who I knew, and if there were any cute girls. I sighed as I realized there weren't many girls present and those that were held little interest for me. My pattern up until that time would be to ask someone out, date them a few times and then break up. I was looking for a girl that was serious and yet exciting. None of the girls I had met fit that description.

And that's when I saw *her*.

I immediately got up from the booth and began to follow her as she walked around the dance floor. "Now that's my type of girl, right there," I thought to myself as I studied her from behind. Lavonne was on the taller side, a thin cute figure, and she was blonde. That immediately caught my attention. Some years back, I considered the characteristics I wanted in the girl I wanted to marry. One of the physical characteristics that I desired was that she would be blonde. Now, I lived in Costa Rica. So, I'm not sure where that thought came from, but it was there and this girl walking gracefully in front of me was blonde. It was just one of the attributes that caught my attention and there were many of them. Oddly, I actually sensed that God had sent her there for me. I watched from a distance as she sat down in a booth with another girl and several other guys. I thought she must be with them, but none of them asked her to dance. I continued to observe her. I simply couldn't take my eyes off her.

I nudged my buddy who had walked over to where I was, "Look at that girl," I said as I nodded my head to where she sat. "I like her."

"Well what are you waiting for? Get over there and ask her to dance," he said giving me a light push in her direction.

It was one thing to admire her from afar, and quite another to act on that impulse. I battled in my mind as I walked over to her. She didn't seem like she was too interested in the guys sharing the booth with her, so I took a deep breath, walked up to her and with all the courage I could muster, introduced myself.

"Will you dance with me?" I asked, extending my hand.

To my surprise and delight she immediately jumped up, accepting my invitation. I couldn't believe my luck. Smiling from ear to ear, I walked her out to the dance floor. As we started dancing, I started talking. It didn't take but a few moments for me to recognize she didn't understand a word I was saying. This beautiful blonde didn't know Spanish.

Communication was an adventure as we spent the rest of the evening dancing, trying to communicate with each other and laughing at our limited language skills. She didn't speak Spanish and I couldn't speak English. We used lots of hand gestures and nods and the evening sped by.

I learned her name was Lavonne. She was from the U.S.A., the state of Oregon and had come to Costa Rica to learn Spanish. She had only been there about a month. I looked back over at the booth where her friends sat and recognized the boys at the table. Then I understood why she was with them. They were part of her host home where she would stay during her year-long high school exchange program.

Although just a year apart in age, because of the way the Costa Rican education system was set up at that time, I was already in my last year of college, while Lavonne was in her last year of high school.

Although communication was pretty tough, she intrigued me. There was something about her that was different. Perhaps her spunk at coming to a foreign country to study, or perhaps it was her engaging smile, and after all she was blonde! We danced the rest of the evening together, and spoke very slowly. Between that and the hand gestures, somehow we seemed to understand each other.

Several days later I saw her again at another disco. I think she was as happy to see me as I was to see her. Her face immediately lit up with a big smile as I walked over to where she was seated. "Do you want to dance?" I asked.

We picked up right where we had left off several days before. Although the language barrier was enormous, there was a comfortable feeling between us. I liked this girl and loved the opportunity to get to know her more. The evening sped by until it was time to leave. As Lavonne and her friends got up to leave, she walked by me and she touched me lightly on the shoulder to say good-bye. Startled by the gesture, my mind started racing. That is something a Costa Rican girl would never have done at that time. It would have been considered extremely forward. But in the next instant, I realized that this must have been a typical, friendly gesture in U.S. culture. Not forward, just friendly. I felt warmed by her gesture and realized I *really* liked this girl—a lot. I learned that she would be in Costa Rica for a year. I made the determination then and there that I wanted to make good use of that time and get to know her better, only I forgot to ask her for her phone number!

I don't think Lavonne was as taken with me at the beginning as I was with her. Maybe she just saw me as a good opportunity to work on her language skills! As I said, she was just as serious about her desire to learn Spanish as I was about my studies in engineering. I think that is one of the things that drew me to her. She had a passion I hadn't seen in the other girls I had dated. Lavonne had a dream and was willing to leave the comfort of her family and home to pursue it. She wasn't afraid to experience new things or places so I was determined to help her experience my culture.

Not long after, my friend Jorge and I were at the city fair when I noticed Lavonne walking toward us. It was a small city and the fair was a big attraction.

"Hey Jorge, I whispered. "Do you have any money on you? I want to invite Lavonne to join us for the bull fight." Although it was only twenty-five cents for the entrance fee, I only had enough for one ticket. I looked expectantly at my friend.

"I've got fifty cents," he responded as he dug into his pocket for his change.

"Will you loan me twenty-five, so I can invite Lavonne to go in with us?" I pleaded.

Jorge responded with a warm smile and a nod. That turned into a very fun but unexpected date.

Lavonne told me later that what she remembered most about that date was that Jorge and I spent most of the time telling jokes back and forth.

"I couldn't understand most of what they said, but I enjoyed being with them and sharing their laughter even if I couldn't understand the jokes!" she explained. "We talked and laughed most of the afternoon as I watched the skill of the Costa Rican bull fighters trying to avoid being run over by the bull. It ranks as one of my favorite memories."

Afterwards, we said good-bye to Jorge and I walked Lavonne home. All the way I tried to work up the courage to give her a kiss and let her know how I felt. As we walked up to the door of her host home, I looked straight into her eyes and made my move. We kissed lightly and then said good night. I thought my heart would beat out of my chest. That was it! I was officially in love!

Over the next several months, Lavonne and I spent most of our "dates" together sitting on the red sofa in the sitting room of her host home talking and getting to know each other. "Dating" in the sense of going out alone all the time wasn't acceptable in our culture. So our time together was spent talking, and enduring the teasing of many kids that were part of Lavonne's host family who enjoyed spying on the "love birds." Because we spent so much time talking, Lavonne's skill in Spanish increased quickly and the language barrier that had been huge at the beginning was becoming less and less as time went by.

With her adventurous spirit, Lavonne wasn't afraid to experience the food and culture of Costa Rica. I remember buying a granadilla, a fruit common to our area, for her to try. It is a roundish oval fruit with a shiny orange skin. The inside is similar to a pomegranate with jelly-like pulp surrounding numerous black edible seeds. Lavonne would try everything at least once. I enjoyed seeing her reaction as she crinkled up her nose and made a face. She was a good sport. I liked to introduce her to local things that she would have never discovered on her own and places such as the mountains and rivers that weren't touristy. You had to be a local to know they were there. Lavonne was always up for a new adventure. It was intriguing to see my country through her eyes. Things that had become commonplace for me took on fresh life as she experienced them for the first time. Her quick laughter and smile also had a way of making things fun.

Before we knew it, there was just a month left before the end of the school year and her to return to the USA. I hadn't really thought ahead to the fact that Lavonne wasn't staying. After all, I'm a guy. I was just enjoying the moment and our friendship, but now reality hit and I couldn't ignore it any longer. Lavonne was going to leave.

"She really is going," I thought to myself. I didn't like the feeling and whether intentional or not, I began to distance myself. It was a selfish thing, I know, but I just knew I didn't want to suffer. So, I started to pull away and create a gap to protect my heart. We argued quite a bit that month, and I was emotionally distant as I worked to build walls around my heart and pull away. I'm sure it hurt Lavonne. I could see it in her eyes, but still I continued. I kept creating distance emotionally until one night I took a more drastic step.

We had spent the evening talking again at her host home and as I stood up to leave I made a decision, "I think we need to end it here," I said. "You're about to leave and obviously this relationship isn't going to go anywhere." The flash of surprise and hurt I read in Lavonne's eyes told me she didn't like my decision. Yet, I didn't want to delay the pain I knew was inevitable. Lavonne and I were both pragmatists and although we really liked each other a lot, we always understood that we should just enjoy the relationship and realize it would probably never be anything further. That wasn't true for some of my friends who got involved with other exchange students. Lavonne and I laughed at those couples who declared they were getting married and truly believed they could have a future together.

While the past few months had been great fun, and the language barrier had diminished significantly, it was apparent, at least in my mind, that the relationship had no future. I had no aspirations of going to the States, and she had no aspirations of staying. It seemed logical to just end it right there. My resolve didn't last long. While my head was pragmatic, my heart had gotten involved.

"Rodolfo is miserable." Miguel, my brother-in-law told Lavonne after he ran into her in the city a few days later. "We have to do something," he told her. Together they planned a "chance" meeting where he invited me to meet him at a coffee shop and Lavonne just "happened" to run into us. I was so excited to see her and immediately we got back together. My brother-in-law had been right. I was miserable and this girl definitely had my heart, but she was still leaving.

A couple of weeks later, Lavonne boarded the plane to return to her home. I said good-bye to her the night before and we exchanged addresses. In my mind it was over, but in reality, it had only just begun.

Chapter 3

TRANSITIONS

The years we are in our teens and early twenties are a period of life that are full of transitions as we encounter crossroad after crossroad. Each one requiring decisions as we move ahead with our lives. While at that age we often think we know everything, we are rarely completely prepared. I now found myself at one of those roads of transition.

After Lavonne returned to the U.S., I closed my mind and my heart to what had been or might have been and went on with my life immersing myself in my studies. The next few weeks were full as I completed my undergraduate collegiate studies and graduated with honors. While I graduated with a B.S. in Engineering, my older sister, Lucrecia also graduated from the University of Costa Rica about the same time as a microbiologist. We were the first in our family to graduate from college and it was a proud moment.

To my surprise, my college asked me to stay on and teach some classes. At just nineteen, I would be the youngest professor they had ever had on staff. I agreed, thrilled to finally have a paycheck coming in. Within just a few months I had been able to save a good bit of money. Life couldn't have gotten much better, but still, if I was honest with myself, I missed Lavonne.

A few weeks later, I received a letter from her in the mail. "Dear Rodolfo, I made it back home safely…." It was a lengthy letter that detailed her return trip and what she was doing now that she was home. It was the first of several letters. Lavonne will tell you it was just a typical letter to let me know she was home safe -- something she would write to any friend. I took it as "she still likes me." It immediately stirred the emotions that I had tried to let die.

More letters followed as we started corresponding back and forth. Lavonne's were lengthy and full of details of her life and family in the States. I wasn't much for writing letters. Again, I'm a guy, and while I did write her back, her lengthy letters received only short responses of three to four sentences which I usually struggled over. But, at least we were communicating. I thoroughly enjoyed receiving her letters, and not long after, she invited me to come to Oregon to visit her that summer. Although I hadn't been working long, I had diligently saved and realized I *could* make the trip. I requested a two-week vacation for the summer, and we immediately began making plans.

Of course, I had learned some about the United States in school, but I had no idea what it was really like. I flew into Los Angeles where Lavonne and her parents and younger brother, David, picked me up. It was the first time I had ever flown. It was exciting in so many ways, but the best was I got to see Lavonne again.

After the plane landed, I was in for my first surprise. The Los Angeles airport was huge compared to the airport I had flown out of in Costa Rica. As I walked out of the gate I saw Lavonne and her family. I gave her a big hug. My English was still so limited that I couldn't even manage, "Hello Mr. and Mrs. Rogelstad," But I offered a big smile as I stretched out my hand. I had met them previously in Costa Rica when they had come to visit Lavonne. That had been an adventure in itself.

At that time Lavonne had already been in Costa Rica a few months when she mentioned her parents were coming to visit. I didn't know what to do with them having never hosted an American family before. That's when my brother Carlos gave me an idea. "Rodolfo, the cabin where my work crew and I stay during the week will be empty. You can take them there." It sounded like a great idea. The price was right—free—and it was located right on the beach. So, I offered to take Lavonne and her family there to show them the sights. The adventure came in getting there.

We boarded the train from the capital, San Jose, and headed to the beach area close to Puntarenas. It was about a four-hour trip. The train was a typical old Costa Rican train, nothing plush at all. At every stop along the way, vendors were waiting on the platform to sell chickens, food, snacks, drinks, etc. When we arrived at our station I grabbed my small bag, but Lavonne's parents each had a large suitcase to carry. "How far is it from here?" They asked as Lavonne translated. "About two kilometers," I responded as we started off down the road. The traffic from the road sped past us, sending a hot cloud of dust swirling around us as we walked. There was no trail of soft grass or dirt, instead we were walking on gravel roads. We walked, and walked and walked.

Lavonne's parents struggled with the suitcases as they wiped the sweat that was trickling down their faces. "How much further is it?" they asked again. "About two kilometers," I responded. Several more times during that trip, they asked me how much further, and each time I responded the same. No matter how far we walked, it was still two kilometers. I really don't know how far we walked in the end, but I *know* it was significantly further than two kilometers!

Finally, we reached the small cabin, which was actually more like an old wood shack. It was a simple bare structure for work crews to sleep. It usually housed guys that were building roads, who worked long hours and needed little more than just a place to eat dinner and crash in bed at night. It was furnished with three or four metal bunk beds, a small kitchen, and absolutely no frills. We only stayed one night…thankfully.

After we arrived and dropped off our luggage, we went down to the beach to a restaurant. After looking at the menu we all ordered hamburgers. When the waitress brought them to our table, there was a large bun on each of our plates, but we had to lift up the bun to find any meat. The actual patty inside was about a fourth of the size of the bun! I never lived down the infamous "no meat beach burgers" and two kilometers walk from that trip. Both provided lots of laughter. Like Lavonne, her parents were adventurous, quick to laugh and seemed to have a good time. I liked them. They were very friendly and never seemed concerned that their daughter was dating someone from another culture or country.

We spent a few days first in California where they introduced me to Disneyland. That's where I had a surprise encounter. You see, in Costa Rica we have no time zones. The entire country is on the same time all year. Plus, we don't have any need for Daylight Savings Time since we are so close to the equator. In Costa Rica the sun sets around 6:30 every day, of every year. It never changes, and we set our dinner meal around that time. It was our very first day in California as they took me around Disneyland. We walked and walked and rode rides and explored. I was starting to get tired and really hungry, but no one said anything about food. Plus, the sun was still up. Yet, my stomach was growling. I couldn't figure out why I was so hungry and finally said something to Lavonne. "What time is it anyway?" I asked. She glanced at her watch, "It's about 8:30," she replied.

Eight-thirty? How could it be eight-thirty at night? The sun was still up. That's when I first learned about time zones and daylight savings time. That was a new concept to me that there could be sunlight after 6:30 p.m. It's like seeing snow for the first time. In the U.S., the sun could stay up past 6:30 p.m.!

The California tour continued as they took me to Universal Studios, and then onto San Francisco, where we drove on the famous Lombard Street and Golden Gate bridge and then through the Redwood Forest before her dad pointed the car toward Oregon and their home. One of the things that impressed me so much was the tall, perfectly shaped pine trees. They really blew me away. We don't have that kind of pine trees in Costa Rica. What we have are a lot of types and shapes of trees, but not the tall perfectly shaped trees. As we drove I saw rows and rows of majestic pines perfectly shaped and beautiful. We continued taking in the scenery and sights on the way to their home. These included Crater Lake in the southern part of Oregon. It was awe inspiring. I had never seen anything like it. I learned that the huge lake was created when a violent eruption triggered the collapse of a volcano that towered nearby. Now the huge crater left behind is fed by rain and snow. It is considered the deepest lake in the United States and because of the way it is fed, perhaps the most pristine on earth.

Enroute to their home, we stopped in the city of Corvallis to tour Oregon State University. I didn't know what to think as we walked into the Industrial Engineering Department. The dean of the department, Dr. James Riggs was there and greeted us warmly. As he introduced himself, I recognized him as the author of one of the engineering books I had studied during college. We shook hands and he talked—mainly to Lavonne's parents since I couldn't speak English—before taking a short tour of the campus. It was impressive. It was my first introduction to an American university campus. Dr. Riggs tried to include me in the conversation and asked me several questions about Costa Rica. He was tall and friendly, with a warm smile. I remember walking around the facility and labs and trying to take it all in. These labs had more equipment, more books, and more research facilities than the ones at my college. It was all very exciting.

When back in the car and on the last leg of the journey to Lavonne's home, I engaged in my newest obsession since arriving in the states. Blowing bubbles. After I arrived, Lavonne's brother had given me a piece of bubble gum. Believe it or not, I had never had bubble gum before, and was fascinated with learning the art of blowing bubbles. I chewed and practiced until my jaws ached, unwilling to give up until I had mastered it! I also learned about trash cans. It may sound funny, but in Costa Rica, at least when I was young, if you had trash you threw it on the ground. There weren't trash cans conveniently available and we were never trained to think that way. During the trip we pulled into a drive-in to get some hamburgers. After finishing my burger, I wadded up the paper, rolled down the window and tossed it out. Lavonne's father evidently saw the paper flying behind the car in his rear-view mirror. "Who threw that paper out?" he asked. I turned and saw Lavonne's face. She was horrified, and then broke out laughing.

"Rodolfo, you can't throw your trash out the window like that. We'll get a ticket," she explained. This country was very different from my own.

After reaching Portland, we drove another twenty miles east to Columbia River Gorge. It is a canyon stretching eighty miles with cascading waterfalls and breathtaking beauty. From there we drove to the Mount Hood Summit. As we went up to the peak I marveled. I had seen pictures of snow, but it was the first time I had actually seen it for myself. I scooped up a handful and tried to make a snowball, but it was brown and had more dirt and ice than snow. The two weeks passed quickly and in no time at all I was to head back to Costa Rica. I had enjoyed the opportunity to get to know Lavonne's family and friends and spend time with her again. Although my English was still minimal, she acted as our translator.

Just hours before I was to head back to the airport I turned to Lavonne and asked, "Would you marry me if I asked you?" It wasn't a formal ask mind you. I was just testing the waters and wanted to know where she was at in the relationship. Maybe this could work after all…

"I don't know. Let me talk with my mom," she replied.

Perhaps she didn't think I was serious, but after talking with her mom she replied, "Mom said it's okay as long as I don't have any doubts. But Rodolfo, I'm not sure. I have some doubts."

Well, to my ears that sounded like a "no" and so we said good-bye for the second time and I boarded the plane. Once again, I felt sure that our relationship was over. How could there be a future ahead for us?

The stewardess closed the door of the jet as I made my way to my seat. It was as if the relationship closed simultaneously.

Back in Costa Rica and teaching again at the Instituto Tecnológico was enjoyable. I loved what I was doing, but I knew this was only a temporary position on my way to something else. I had a full life ahead, and like most young adults, had high hopes and dreams. Deep in my heart, I wanted to own my own business. How it could happen or what it would be, I had no idea. However, the thought was there like a seed buried deep in the ground.

I continued to receive long letters from Lavonne sharing with me about her life. I began to date other girls, and would occasionally tell Lavonne about them, in my short replies. She was entering college and would be attending Pacific Lutheran University in Tacoma, Washington just a few hours from her home. I continued my work as a professor at the school… with that seed, my dream for a business, growing without me even knowing.

At some point during that first year of teaching in the institute, I was told I would receive a one-year scholarship to study abroad. After teaching for a year, I was excited at the opportunity to once again further my education. "You need to start sending out applications as soon as possible," said Ing. Raul Mena, (Ing. is a title and stands for engineer in Spanish). He was the director of the Industrial Production Engineering department. He was also my boss.

Immediately, I thought of Oregon State University where I had met Dr. Riggs. "I actually toured Oregon State University and met Dr. James Riggs who wrote one of our text books," I explained to him. The news was well received, and the staff actually encouraged me to apply and see if I could be accepted. My head was spinning with all the new developments, and I quickly wrote Lavonne to inform her of what was happening. I completed several applications including the one to Oregon State. I was accepted into their Industrial Engineering master's degree program not long afterwards. I would start classes January 1978. But there was a problem. I still couldn't speak English!

31

Chapter 4

UNBELIEVABLE OPPORTUNITIES

Have you ever been in a dark room fumbling for the light switch? When your hand finds the switch and you flip it up, the room floods with light. I learned that walking through life, without God's wisdom, is like walking through a dark room and not turning on the light switch. The chances are, if we take a walk in the dark, we're going to stumble and get hurt.

Times of transition, more than any other time in our lives, cause us to ponder and consider our future and what decision will we make. They create questions such as: Should I continue my education? What school should I attend? What job should I apply for and take? Who should I marry? Is this person the right one? Should I move to a different location? Should I change jobs? How will I be able…? Each day of our lives we make decisions. Most come naturally, but still can affect our lives. For example, if we are driving down the road and are in a car accident. What if we had made the decision to leave the house twenty minutes earlier? Or what if we had made the decision to take a different route? We often don't think twice about those type of daily decisions and yet they can change the course of our lives. How much more the weighty decisions of life which require more thought and wisdom?

During this time, both Lavonne and I were walking through life as if it were a dark room making decisions from our head, but without true wisdom. For true wisdom, I have learned comes from God. So, in many ways, we were simply stumbling around in the dark. It was a recipe to stumble and fall.

We both had an understanding of God, but little more. I had been raised in the Catholic Church and Lavonne in a Lutheran Church, but to be honest neither of us took our faith seriously. So, we were walking through life like most people, trying to do our best and hoping for the best. But who wants to live life guessing and always wondering if the decision we make is right? That can lead to a life of regrets and "what ifs." "What if I made a different decision?" "What if I did/didn't marry this person?" "What if I had finished my education?" "What if I had taken a different job?" When we live life like that, we are living as if everything depends on us. It does, because we haven't turned it over to the One who created us and has a plan for us. What a weight we carry!

I know in my heart there was a deep hunger for God. I didn't understand it at that time, but it was there. My heart yearned for truth as I sat in Mass. Each time the priest read from scripture, there was something there. And so I prayed and asked God questions. I still didn't know if He was real, and yet in my heart I wanted to believe He was. I had questions. Lots of them. Why are we on the earth? Where do we go after death? Is heaven real? Is there a God? If there is, who is He and why can't we see Him? Is the Bible true?

Perhaps you are in that place as you read this. You wonder if God is real? Perhaps you don't believe there is a God. But I can tell you as I look back over my life, it is clear He was guiding and protecting me even before I truly knew Him or surrendered my life to Him.

His guiding hand was right there as my employer offered me a full one-year scholarship to continue my education in the States.

I shook my head as I considered what had just happened, and considered the recent events that had brought yet another transition to my life. I was given a full scholarship from the Instituto Tecnológico, encouraged to further my education and attend Oregon State University, near where Lavonne and her family lived. As impossible as it all seemed, on top of that, my application had been accepted. It seemed too good to be true.

I had only four months before I was to leave for Oregon State University. That meant four months to learn English. I had to get serious and fast. I searched and discovered a program in Costa Rica that claimed that once students completed the one hundred twenty-hour program, they would be fluent English speakers. That's what I needed and I immediately enrolled. One hundred and twenty hours later, I still couldn't speak a lick of English! Now with only four weeks before I was to leave, my chest tightened at the thought of how I could take master's level courses in a second language that I didn't even understand.

I arrived at Oregon State University in January 1978, little prepared for my introduction to the English language or the weather. It took only one day to realize my wardrobe wasn't suitable for the cold Oregon winter. In Costa Rica, the temperatures often hover around seventy degrees Fahrenheit in the mountains, but around ninety degrees or more in the beach areas. The coldest it ever gets, even in the winter (or rainy season) is the low sixties. I was walking around in a short-sleeved t-shirt in forty-degree weather. I didn't even own a heavy coat and shivered as I made my way across campus. "This is what it must feel like to live in a refrigerator," I thought to myself.

I was immediately enrolled in two English classes, but I also asked if I could audit two of the engineering classes. Dr. Riggs graciously agreed, and that's when the hard work really began.

The English classes were hard enough, but sitting through lectures on engineering and the specific vocabulary used in those lectures, was over-whelming. My schedule each day consisted of going to class, and then studying with little food or sleep. I spent hours with the engineering text book opened beside me along with a Spanish-to-English dictionary. I worked to translate and study each chapter before going to class. I took notes as best I could during the lecture, and then headed back to my room immediately afterwards where I would go back over the chapter line-by-line and word-by-word translating again so I could understand. The English labs were easier and extremely helpful. In the labs I could listen to the audio over and over again. Hitting rewind and play, rewind and play as many times as I needed. For three months, I studied like this and still was barely able to understand the professor as he lectured. But somewhere between the third and fourth month, I realized I had a general grasp of the lectures as the professor taught. Instead of being able to focus on the few words I did understand, now I only had to focus on the few words I didn't understand. It was a huge breakthrough. Still, it took me almost the entire year to feel somewhat comfortable with the English language.

Finally, the day came for a test. I was tempted not to take it, but I knew I needed to try. The professor had so much compassion toward me. "Rodolfo, you are auditing the class, you don't have to take the test," he said. I shook my head as I sat down, pencil in hand. I had made my decision, and I was determined to do my best. There were only five problems on the test and we had forty-five minutes to complete them. That may sound like plenty of time, but even the sharpest guy in the class could only complete three before time was called. The tests are made to see what you have in you, so they are created with the intent that the student won't be able to finish. For the first round of tests, I still had to use my Spanish-English dictionary to translate the problems and then do the calculations. I was still working on the first problem when time was called. I was frustrated.

I knew I could do the work, but I needed more than forty-five minutes. After class I walked up to the professor, "I only finished one problem," I explained. "May I take the test back to my apartment and work on it?" He agreed. I worked and worked translating and then working the problems. It was hard work, but ten hours later, I finished it. The next day I handed it back to the professor. "Can you check it?" I asked. He probably laughed, after all this was an audit class, but he did it. It was important to me. Once I received the corrected paper back, it would show me where I was wrong and where I needed to improve. In the end, the professor gave me a "B" for the class. I smiled as I looked at the grade. It was a hard-earned grade and a miracle. I didn't recognize just how much of a miracle until later.

During that year I saw Lavonne several times. She was enrolled in Pacific Lutheran University in Tacoma, Washington which was about a four-hour drive away. After the end of the first semester, her parents invited me to spend the summer with them. It was nice to have the break from the intense studying regimen. Lavonne and I got along well, although I doubt I was as attentive to her that summer as I had been the year before. I saw no future for us, and so intentionally put some distance between us. I enjoyed getting to know her friends and attending parties. I was also mesmerized by a craft project that she worked on all summer. It was a latch rug. It was a kit with a design painted on the plastic frame. Lavonne spent hours hooking the pre-cut yarn into the latch hook, and pulling it through the frame until it hooked into place. Hundreds of small pieces of yarn came together to create a beautiful design of a sailboat out on the water. Before we knew it, summer break was over. We loaded up the car to drop Lavonne back off at school and then the same for me. Although my English level was higher than the previous semester, it still took an intense amount of concentration and translating each chapter of the text books in engineering for me to understand the concept and do well in the class. Yet I was determined, and the passion I had for learning served me well as I pressed ahead.

As the time neared for the end of the semester, so would conclude my scholarship. Part of the requirements of the scholarship was that I would return to my college in Costa Rica and teach for two years. So, I had to n to my teaching job to fulfill that two-year teaching commitment. Lavonne and I talked about the relationship again, and together we decided to break it off. We both felt that the strain the distance would put on the relationship would be too severe.

Now at the airport waiting for my plane, I took her hands and looked into her eyes. I wondered if this was as hard for her as it was for me. "You'll be married within two years," I told her. That turned out to be a prophetic word, but neither Lavonne nor I could see past the present.

It was with a sad but practical heart that I boarded the plane, taking with me the beautiful hand-crafted rug Lavonne had worked on all summer. She gave it to me as a surprise—a memento of a miraculous year in the United States. Lavonne and I said good-bye once again as I headed back to Costa Rica.

I immersed myself back into my teaching position and my students, partly because that was my nature to give 100% to the task at hand. It was also to take my mind off of the relationship I had left behind. I was doing pretty well with it, until I received a letter from Lavonne.

In her typical newsy fashion, Lavonne told me all about her family, what had been happening in recent months and the big news that she was planning to continue her Spanish studies, but this time in Spain. I relished the fact that she wanted to keep in touch and share what she was doing, and so the letter writing between us resumed. Her lengthy letters were followed by my short responses.

I buried myself in my work for the rest of 1979 and into 1980, fulfilling my pay-back teaching year to my school. During that time, I also organized a National Industrial Engineering Seminar. I invited Dr. Riggs to come and give lectures to all of the Costa Rican industrial engineers. The seminar was well attended and quite a success. It also furthered my relationship with Dr. Riggs, who had really taken me under his wing during my time at Oregon State.

As I continued to look at my future, while I didn't have a complete plan, there were certain things I did know. While I enjoyed my teaching position and had found great favor with the school, my ultimate goal was to have my own business, so I strategized what that might include and the options available. I didn't know where to start, but the desire burned within me. I also determined that I loved Lavonne and wanted to let her know how much I cared for her. Perhaps we could make the relationship work after all.

I decided that I would create a latch rug for her, as she had done for me. The only problem was the kits to make the rugs as Lavonne had used were not available in Costa Rica. The project was no simple task. I had to first create a wooden frame, and then hammer nails in every quarter of an inch all the way around the square frame. Next, I wound a string first horizontally and then vertically from nail to corresponding nail and glued them in place to create the base of the rug. I had no precut yarn to use, and so had to create my own little system using a broom stick. First, I cut a small notch along the broom stick. Then each piece of yarn had to be wrapped around the stick and cut with a pair of scissors at the precut notch. It was an elaborate process. I hoped Lavonne would appreciate the thought and labor of love that went into the creation of her rug. I planned to have it finished in time to ship it to her in Spain for her birthday.

Excited, I wrote her a long letter this time. Lavonne loved longer letters and so I applied myself to really share details of what was happening in my life as she did for me in her letters. In the middle of the letter I let her know how much I loved her and that I couldn't get her out of my mind. I wasn't prepared for her response.

"Rodolfo, I love you as well, but I have some concerns about our relationship..." It turns out that most of her concerns were with my communication, or lack thereof. While Lavonne had always shared extensively in both her letters and when we were together, it was much harder for me. It wasn't my nature. As a result, my letters were usually short and lacked details. That wasn't all. She also pointed out that when I was upset, that I

39

typically shut down and didn't want to talk about it. She was right. I kept things bottled up inside and wasn't always as attentive as she needed. I pondered what she said, and I knew I could change. I would change!

I immediately picked up paper and pen and responded with a long letter assuring Lavonne that I would work on those areas and change as much as needed. I also let her know that I had a special surprise that would arrive in Spain in time for her birthday. Lavonne wrote back immediately and thought that the surprise was that I was planning to fly down to see her. "Well, why not?" I thought to myself. I immediately checked on flight availability and price and booked my ticket. I smiled at the thought of seeing Lavonne. I would hand-deliver the birthday rug and show her just how attentive and communicative I could be.

It was Easter week, also known as Holy week, when I landed in Seville where Lavonne lived. Occurring on the last week of Lent, immediately before Easter the holiday brought visitors from all over who came to partic-ipate in the daily festivities and processions. Because of the many visitors, by the time I arrived I couldn't find a single hotel room available. The family Lavonne was staying with would not allow me to spend the night in the same house where she lived, and so Lavonne tried fruitlessly to find somewhere that I could stay, but with no success. There was no vacancy anywhere.

"Don't worry, I can find somewhere to stay," I told her that evening after I arrived. We stayed and talked together until almost midnight, at which time I said goodnight. As she shut the door, I turned and started to walk down the street. I had no idea where I would go. As I walked, I came to an area in which many people had simply laid down on the sidewalk to sleep. At least I wasn't the only one who found themselves in this situation. I determined that if I was going to have to sleep outside, that it would be safer to do so with several people around me than off by myself. So, I picked a spot between two strangers and laid down on the sidewalk. The rough, uneven cobblestones were very uncomfortable and no matter how I turned, I couldn't fall into a deep sleep.

40

At some point during the night, a loud noise awoke me. I watched as all the people around me who had been lying on the sidewalk got up and began rushing toward some large gates. I had no idea what was happening. I continued to watch until a few minutes later, when the large gates swung open and dozens of people rushed inside. I made my way over to the gates and peered inside and then realized this was the train station. Once the gates had opened the individuals had rushed in to claim one of the many vacant benches for a bed. By the time I got there, every bench was already taken except one. That one was a circular bench and had a structural pole that ran through the middle of the bench. It was a little awkward, but better than the rough cobblestone. I laid down to sleep. It worked fairly well, except when I felt the need to roll over. The only way to accomplish the feat was to get up and walk around the pole and lay down on the other side. It was a memorable first night in Spain. Fortunately, I was able to find a hotel room for the remainder of my trip.

I presented the hand-crafted rug to Lavonne for her birthday and we celebrated it together by drinking sangria and eating "tapas." We spent the next few days exploring the city among the crowds of visitors. Seville is famous for its Holy Week processions, which happened to take place the week I was there. The streets were flooded with people. It was quite the event. The women were dressed up and I noticed many wore a beautiful black lace shawl known as a "mantilla." It was pulled up over their head and shoulders and fastened onto their hair with an ornate comb. One significant part of Holy Week was the processions or parade of people who walked down the street carrying large statues of either saints, the Virgin Mary or Christ as they shouldered the weight together carrying it across boards on their shoulders as an offering of penance. Some rode on horseback in bright silk robes. Others just walked alongside.

In addition to the processions were other traditions. As she had done in Costa Rica, Lavonne had immersed herself in the culture and activities of the area. Not only did this show in her fluency of the language, which had increased significantly, but also in her ability to join in the culture.

She displayed this for me several times during that week by joining in the popular dance known as the Sevillana.

"La Sevillana" is a type of street flamenco that is performed regularly everywhere, even in the middle of the street. Everyone will just begin to dance it. Men and women of all ages, families, and even an entire town will participate. It is performed at their fiestas, but also just as recreation during the entire year. It is rather complicated, with four parts to learn and Lavonne had mastered it. She joined in as the streets filled and the music started, unwilling to miss something that so marked their culture. There was so much activity around us and the entire week was like one big party.

On an impulse on the crowded streets, I stopped, took Lavonne in my arms and dipped her back giving her a big kiss. "Will you marry me?" I asked. Lavonne's face flushed slightly crimson as people walked by and stared at us. I had taken her completely by surprise. "Yes," she responded as I took her hand and we headed on down the street. We were still on the same road, surrounded by crowds of people and yet it felt, in my mind as if we were alone, I was so elated. But I realized I wanted to give her a proper proposal.

Later that week we toured the historic Alhambra castle located in the city of Granada. Known for its breathtaking Mudéjar style architecture of carved stucco and Arabic inscriptions, it consisted of beautiful courtyards filled with sparkling water fountains and gardens. It was almost magical. It was the perfect place for a "proper" proposal. This time with the setting of the beautiful castle around us, I asked Lavonne to be my wife. She smiled as she once again accepted my proposal, but has never let me forget that I asked her to marry me in a castle that was also known for its harems!

I returned to Costa Rica after our short visit together in Spain with a deep satisfaction about our relationship. It felt right…like it was destiny. I remember telling my mom and the rest of the family of our engagement, "You remember that girl, the gringa?" I asked. "Well, I think we are getting married." My mom and siblings were happy for me. They knew Lavonne a little bit from when she had studied in Costa Rica. She was so bubbly and warm to them and they had accepted her even back then. The only problem was two months later as Lavonne began traveling during her summer break. She would often call me since she was traveling and I didn't know how to contact her. I remember Mom or one of my sisters would call me with "Oh Rodolfo, Lavonne is calling you from Germany, or Lavonne is calling you from Norway, or Lavonne is calling you from Seville." It seemed she was always calling from a new location. Mom laughed but I think was only half joking when she finally said, "Hijo (son), are you sure you can afford that girl?"

So that led to the other big question in my life, the direction for my career and how to provide for myself and my family. That next decision sent me on a path that I never expected.

Chapter 5

A GUIDING HAND

Have you ever had the sense that things were going to work out? That something was actually guiding you in the direction you should go? Some call it providence. Others call it luck. At that time in my life, I knew I needed wisdom and I certainly wasn't willing to trust my future to luck.

After returning to Costa Rica from the short visit to see Lavonne, I began to contemplate the rest of my future. Now that it was settled that Lavonne and I would get married, that was simply one piece of the puzzle. Would we live in her country, or mine? What direction should I go with my career? One thing was certain and that was I knew I wanted to finish the master's degree I had already started at Oregon State University. In order to do that, I would need to quit my teaching job. But where would the tuition money come from? I did the calculations and would need approximately $10,000. I didn't have it, and taking out a loan for it didn't feel right. I was uncertain and not knowing what else to do, I decided to pray. "God, if you're out there, please help me and show me what to do." As I finished the prayer, a heavenly peace descended on me, and I knew I was to turn in my application to Oregon State. I didn't know how I was going to swing it regarding tuition, but I followed through with the feeling and mailed it off.

It didn't take long for me to receive the acceptance letter for my return to Oregon State. Before I had time to begin to fret over how I would get the tuition money, my boss walked into my office to talk.

"Professor Blanco, we have just received an offer from the United States Embassy to fund one of our teachers for a year's study in the United States to work on their post graduate degree. We've discussed it and decided that if you want the scholarship, it is yours."

I couldn't believe my ears. "Yes, of course I want it!" I replied without hesitation.

"Then you will need to begin the application process as soon as possible," he replied.

"I won't need to do that," I informed him.

I could see the confusion on Ing. Arturo Cespedes' face as he hurried over to my desk. He was the new head of the engineering department. I pulled out the acceptance letter from Oregon State in my top drawer and handed it to him. I watched as he read it. He was speechless—and impressed.

"Then it's all set," Ing. Cespedes said as he stood, shook my hand and left.

What had just happened? A warm sensation flooded over me as I thanked God for His provision. It felt like a blanket had wrapped around me. I had never had that sensation before of the complete knowledge that there was a God, and He was taking care of me.

I immediately called Lavonne to let her know. We decided to get married the following summer, and I made plans to return to the USA to complete my degree. It was late summer of 1980 as I stepped foot back onto campus. It felt good to be back and this time, with more English under my belt, it wasn't so hard. I studied hard and worked hard. Lavonne and I called back and forth often. In fact, we talked so often that it was getting quite expensive and painful on the budget. (Note to reader: Long distance at that time was expensive!) So, we made the decision to limit our phone calls to once a day. However, after the first official "once-a-day" phone call, we started cheating with "surprise" phone calls. This snowballed the budget right back to where we had been originally!

So, we decided to move the wedding up from June to December. As soon as the semester finished, I headed to Portland to help prepare for the wedding. We were married in her home church, Milwaukie Lutheran, by her pastor. We also invited a Catholic priest to be part of the ceremony, so that my mom would feel we were actually married!

Usually it is the bride or groom that are nervous, but I have to say, I think the priest was more nervous than either of us. This was one of his first weddings and definitely his first performed in a Lutheran church! Beautiful Christmas decorations gave the church a warm seasonal glow, and we enjoyed a wonderful reception with Latin dancing and delicious food. After the wedding, Lavonne transferred from her university in Tacoma to be with me and finished her degree and student teaching at Oregon State as well. Everything seemed to be falling into place.

A few months later, just as we were both about to graduate, we learned she was pregnant! We were ecstatic. As graduation neared, I realized that I needed two additional classes to complete the degree. I went to my major professor to ask if the two classes I had audited that first year could be applied to my transcript since in the end he had given me a "B." After consideration the school agreed and I had the necessary credit hours for completion. With my master's degree in Industrial Engineering almost in hand, we began to plan our return to Costa Rica where I would fulfill a two-year teaching commitment at El Instituto Tecnológico. I wasn't sure what step I would take after that was completed, but for now it didn't matter. We would have our first home and our first child together as we walked into this new season, and I was at peace.

I had purchased a Honda Civic during my time in Oregon. I used the money I had saved from working, plus what I had when I sold my car in Costa Rica. When I combined the two amounts I had enough for a brand-new Honda Civic. I loved that car. At that time in Costa Rica they charged a tax of 300% on any new car purchase. So, if a car cost $10,000 then the actual cost would be $40,000 with $30,000 of that going to taxes. Gasoline was in short supply and this was one way to keep the automobile population curbed. As you can imagine, it made it tough for most people to purchase a car. At that time only one in ten Costa Ricans owned a car. But there was a law that allowed for anyone who spent a year or more studying abroad and who had obtained a post-graduate degree, to be able to bring a car into the country tax free. I knew I needed to take advantage of that incentive and keep my Honda.

Lavonne and I made plans to drive the car all the way to Costa Rica, but once my brothers heard our plan they asked us to reconsider. Driving through Nicaragua and El Salvador wasn't safe at that time.

"It's too risky. We will meet you if you decide to do it," they said. "But why not look at shipping it over?"

The cheapest fare available was to ship from Miami, Florida. That got our minds thinking. We decided we could ship it from Miami to Costa Rica. We could drive through California first to stop and see her family there, and then see some sights and friends as we made our way to Miami and out of the country. It also gave me an opportunity to stop at a company that made microcomputers.

During my last year in the master's program at OSU, my major professors went to Rockwell International on a program to learn about the newly invented microcomputer. The company donated sixteen to the school which the professor brought back with him upon his return. The only stipulation the company made with the donation was that they had to be used in engineering. I had tremendous favor with Professor Mike Inoue. He sat down with me after his return and offered me the use of one of the computers. "This is for your thesis," he said as he handed it to me. I had no idea how to use it, or how it would become my thesis paper, but I was about to learn. During that year I read, studied, and learned everything I could about the microcomputer, CPU's, boards, etc. and how I could use it in engineering. I completed my thesis paper on "Applications of Micro Processors in Engineering" on the use of those small machines, which was considered cutting edge technology at that time. After graduating and before we left Oregon, I went to say goodbye to Professor Inoue. He had attended our wedding and had even paid for us to attend a Marriage Encounter weekend as a wedding present. He had one more present for me before I left.

"I called Rockwell International after reading your thesis paper about their microcomputer. It was phenomenal. I asked them if they would donate one for you to continue your work and they agreed."

I couldn't believe it! "Thank you, Professor Inoue. This is going to help me a lot," I responded with gratitude.

So, after stopping to see Lavonne's family in the bay area in San Francisco, we went to pick up the donated computer at Rockwell. Little did I realize, but as the tech handed me the computer, he had just handed me my future.

Chapter 6

THE HONDA AND A NEW HOME

We finally arrived in Miami after leaving Oregon almost two weeks before. We had stayed with family and friends along the way as we still had little money from living as students the last couple of years. Once we drove the car to the dock and filled out the paperwork, we had two options. The first was the most economical and the wisest option, but it required us to wait three days for the export papers to be cleared before we left. Otherwise they would have to mail the paperwork to us in Costa Rica before we could pick up the vehicle at the port. What you may not know is that many of the streets in Costa Rica don't even have names and so many of the houses don't have addresses. Nobody mails anything to Costa Rica unless they have a solid address. Also, if the paperwork on my Honda got lost or didn't reach us, we wouldn't be able to pick up the car. Let me tell you, you certainly don't want to leave a car at the docks in Costa Rica very long. It may disappear. So, we made the decision to wait for the paperwork stateside. Hotels, especially the ones near the airport, were expensive. What it would cost us to stay in a hotel for those two or three nights equated to what we would pay for a refrigerator and other necessities for our new home. So, with little money in hand I had the brilliant idea that we could stay in the airport for those three days while we waited and save money.

While it sounded like a good idea at the time, it didn't take long to figure out that staying in the airport long-term is no fun. The first day we purchased a ticket for the city bus and rode around all day and explored. That was fun enough and got us out of the airport, but by the time we got back we discovered that all of the chairs had been taken as overnight passengers waiting for flights like we were had staked their claim to three or four chairs each earlier in the day. That first night we slept on the carpet. It was so noisy and uncomfortable. We had no pillow or blanket, just a backpack to put under our head. Our aching backs let us know that we needed a better plan for the next night. The next day passed painfully slow, and by late afternoon we had to lay claim to some chairs that would serve as our bed for the evening to try to get some sleep. Very little sleep, I might add. The hard-plastic chairs, although better than the carpet, were less than comfortable. Lavonne, in her first trimester of pregnancy, had an even more difficult time trying to find a comfortable position. Pregnancy and mornings also don't go well together.

The last morning before we flew out, we were more than ready to get on that plane and get out of the airport. We went to one of the restaurants for breakfast and to kill some time. We had just finished when Lavonne was hit with a wave of nausea. "Rodolfo, I feel sick. I don't think I'm going to make it to the bathroom." Just as she stood up, she lost it right on the table. I've never seen a place clear so quickly as people jumped from their seats to pay their bill and get out of there. By the time it was all cleaned up and we had paid our bill, the restaurant was completely empty. Oops!

The rest of the trip was uneventful and safe. Lavonne and I found housing near my school and settled in. I started teaching that fall. It was a very challenging yet rewarding job for me. I taught classes in motion and time studies, work measurement, and production control. My biggest challenge was that I was teaching from book knowledge rather than personal experience. The students often asked me, "Have you done this? What is it like?" I did my best to teach what I had been taught, but I knew I still had much to learn along the way.

The next two years sped by quickly. Mariana was born in April that first year and filled our lives with her joy. I was also able to organize a second National Engineering Seminar similar to the one I had done a couple of years before, but this time I invited Professor Mike Inoue, the same professor who had been instrumental in getting the microcomputer donated to me. He agreed to come give the lectures and I was glad for the opportunity to see him again. During his time at the seminar he approached me with an offer. "Rodolfo, I have a book I am writing with another engineer. It is almost completed, but we would like it to be translated into Spanish. Would you join us in this endeavor and be willing to write a chapter in the book and then translate it all into Spanish?" The book was entitled, "Quality Circles" which was a huge buzz-word back then. It was about the miracle of the Japanese industrial revolution that was taking place. Mike graciously gave me co-authorship of the book for that one chapter and the translation work and included my name on the cover and with the publisher. The royalties I received from the book paid our airfare for Lavonne, Mariana and I to take a trip back to Oregon to see her family.

I should have been content, even excited with some of the things that were happening in my life, but instead by the end of that second year of teaching, I was unsettled. I still had that drive to start my own business and had already tried several things, always looking for that niche, but none was a fit.

One of the businesses I started was making carrot cakes. For Lavonne's birthday that year I baked a carrot cake from scratch. Friends and family raved about that cake, which got the wheels turning. Maybe baking carrot cakes was my niche. I made a few cakes and then Lavonne and I went to several of the fancier restaurants in the area offering this "amazing" cake. We started getting orders! Immediately we went out to buy the ingredients and supplies to start production and expand our orders. At that time, we were living in a small house we rented. The oven had three temperature settings, but only one setting worked—high. That made it extremely challenging to get the cakes to turn out correctly without burning them and made the house unbearably hot as the oven ran constantly. Another challenge was that one of the primary ingredients in a carrot cake is grated carrots which was all done by hand. I soon grew weary of the task of grating and elicited Lavonne's help. She took over the grating, but it didn't take long until she was ready to be done with the monotonous chore as well. Finally, we hired a girl to come into our home and do nothing but grate carrots all day. In reality it should have solved our problem, but the girl was an incessant talker. She talked from the moment she walked through the door until she walked out hours later. Much of what she said made absolutely no sense and as she grated carrots, her talking grated on our ears. We finally sent her home and closed the cake baking business.

Always the visionary, it wasn't long before I stumbled on another business idea. This time, I was certain that this would be the idea that launched my dream for a business that would support us. The idea came after my sister told me of yet another break in at their house in a new housing project. She and her husband lived nearby and had just built a home in a new division. The only problem was that the new homes attracted thieves and already they had been broken into several times. As I considered her dilemma, I recognized I could help. During my master's degree studies I had learned a lot about electronics and wiring. I decided to take on the challenge of designing an alarm system and use my sister's house as the test for the first prototype.

The first several attempts failed and resulted in a considerable number of burned out transistors, diodes and resistors. But finally, after much trial and error, I had created a system that seemed to work. I installed a system in my sister's home and another one in a friend's home. The next day I received a call from a rather irate friend. "Rodolfo, your alarm went off at three in the morning!" he exclaimed. The only problem was there were no intruders. When the alarm went off, he scrambled out of bed and fumbled around in search of the gun he had hidden in the bedroom. He searched the premises inside and out, but there was no evidence of any intruder. It was a false alarm. I drove over that day to check the system, but could find nothing wrong. I made a few minor adjustments and then called my friend to let him know it was fixed. But it wasn't. The next morning the alarm triggered again, but this time at four in the morning. Once again my friend shot out of bed in search of an intruder. Once again it was a false alarm. But his wasn't the only alarm that went off. My sister called me later that morning to inform me that her alarm had gone off during the night as well. In fact, it was the alarm that alerted the burglars in her area and drew them to her house later that night. They stole several items, as well as the alarm system which they ripped out of the ceiling. I sighed as I scratched that failed attempt off the business wish list. But my desire to have my own business hadn't diminished. I just didn't know what it was.

Amidst all of the failed business startups I had continued teaching at the Instituto Tecnológico. The longer I taught, the more the frustration built up. I was frustrated that I had never experienced much of what I taught the students. I was full of book knowledge, but like my father, I liked to put things together and see how they worked. I knew it was time to quit my job at the institute and finally get my hands dirty and gain real work experience. With Lavonne's full support, I applied to several jobs. It wasn't long before I had the job of operations manager at the United Fruit Company. It required that we pack up and move to the small town of Coto 47 located near the Panama border. The 16,000-acre palm oil plantation was actually a small community. The company provided housing for its employees and the two-story structures were built in a semi-circle on the property. The upstairs was our housing and the underneath was like an open patio area. I soon discovered why the homes were built in that manner.

It was a challenging yet rewarding job as I managed quality control, and the production data, and reporting for the company. But the move had taken us to a lower elevation and the climate completely different than the comfortable seventy-degree weather we were used to up in the mountains. The locals at this new place often said that they had only two seasons in Coto 47: hot and hotter. The heat and humidity were unrelenting and quickly took their toll. Lavonne was now pregnant with our second child and taking care of Mariana, who was a toddler. Our home had no air-conditioning, which left Mariana cranky and Lavonne tired as the temperatures hovered over the hundred-degree mark year-round. The only relief was to try to capture a cooler breeze at night as we went out onto the open patio area. It took us at least two to three months to adjust and even then, I didn't want anyone to touch me; it was so uncomfortably hot. Eventually we were able to save enough money to purchase a small window unit air-conditioner. It was a blessed relief from the intense heat and needless to say, our time outside on the patio to catch the hot breeze ceased as we all piled into that one room to keep cool.

Later that year, Lavonne gave birth to our second daughter, Diana Melissa. Although neither Lavonne nor I had understood what it was to be surrendered to the Lord yet, we wanted our children to be baptized. We did not attend church much of the time. The primary reason was that the plantation and our home was located in the middle of the jungle. We did join my mom for mass when we visited her in Cartago, but that was about the extent of our religious exposure. We visited the local Catholic church in our city and arranged for the girls' baptism. Even as we attended that service, I left wanting more. I was hungry for truth, for answers. It was much as before when I served as an altar boy. Each time I left feeling as if I had been given crumbs rather than true sustenance. It left me hungry, but for what, I didn't know.

I was restless, not only for answers, but once again I knew we needed to make a change. I had worked at the plantation for two years, but Lavonne and I both were antsy. While I was learning actual skills in my area of degree and was making good pay in my managerial position, now with two kids and travel back and forth to Oregon to see Lavonne's family, we were actually moving lower on the scale toward reaching our financial goals. The exchange rate and inflation added to the dilemma, and we had to look at the facts that my earning power would be greater in the States rather than Costa Rica.

While that wasn't a hard change for Lavonne, it took me awhile to get used to the idea. I would have to communicate in English constantly, which was a rather overwhelming thought at the time. Prior to this we spoke Spanish in our home. So while Lavonne had become completely fluent in my language, I was still unable to speak in English. But if I truly desired to one day own my own business, the opportunities were much greater in the U.S. than if we remained in Costa Rica.

Eventually we made the decision to uproot our family once again. I reached out to my friends and former professors at Oregon State University. They were instrumental in helping me to land my first job on U.S. soil. At least temporarily we would live with Lavonne's family until we could get established on our own. It was February, 1986 when we finally made the move. We sold everything, said goodbye to my family and left Costa Rica with our two kids and only two suitcases of belongings. I also left behind the name Rodolfo. At that point, if I was going to live in the US, I needed a name that people could pronounce and not to be asked how to spell it all the time. So I began going by Rudy. We also left one more thing behind—my precious little Honda. Although, the fact that we sold it used for even more than the original purchase price somehow helped ease the sting as I said good-bye not only to my car, but to the last thing that was familiar to me.

What was I doing?

Chapter 7

BUT I JUST BECAME CATHOLIC!

My father had instilled in me an important lesson. Work hard and do your best and it will pay off in the long run. I saw that philosophy proven true as I applied myself to my education. Now it was time to apply that to the work force.

The move to the United States was a good move for us. It allowed Lavonne to be closer to her family, and provided opportunities that we would not have experienced had we stayed in my country.

The desire for my own business just wouldn't go away, and so I decided to do something about it. "God (for by now I did believe He existed), I'll give you ten years to do something with my life. I want my own business, but I don't know what to do. Will you help me?" I figured ten years was plenty of time for God to do His thing. If He couldn't get it done in that amount of time, then I figured I would take over from there. In essence, I had just given God permission to take over that part of my life and I was in for a ride I never expected. Within a couple of months of our arrival, I accepted a job in Spokane, Washington with the Kaiser Aluminum Company. I was one of eight industrial engineers. It was a good, solid company and even with the move, we were still just five and a half hours from her parents.

My position was oversight of special projects. I handled the tracking of quality control samples and implemented bar code reading systems for real time data reporting. Overall, I enjoyed the job and the pay. The salary was significantly higher than what I had made in my previous job in Costa Rica. With this new salary, we were able to purchase our first home. Although it was small, to us it was like a castle. It was a brand-new structure with a backyard where the girls could safely play. It also had a large unfinished basement. For the first time in my life, I felt content as I looked out from our backyard to a view of some majestic pine trees. Sometimes it still felt like a dream that this home was really ours. Then a new thought came to me. "This is the place we will retire!" But almost immediately, it was followed by that nudging feeling inside that I was made to do something else.

I had been learning the aluminum industry and working for Kaiser for approximately one year when I learned something new about the industry. It can be volatile. Aluminum prices, like the stock market, go up and down. When it's up, everything is good, but when it's down, our jobs could be in jeopardy. Lavonne was now pregnant with our third child and busy with our two girls. So along with our growing family, I also had a mortgage payment and needed this job. About that time, I started to hear comments that made me nervous such as, "Uh oh, aluminum prices are down. The spending freeze is on. Watch out, layoffs will be coming next."

As the "new kid" on the block, the last of the eight engineers hired, I knew that I would be the first to go if layoffs started. Then one day my worst fears were confirmed as my boss called me over to talk. "Rudy, aluminum prices are way down right now," he said. "They're too low. We've been asked to scale way, way back in the engineering department. What that means is we're going to have to cut it in half to just four engineers. I'm sorry, but you need to get prepared for when we get that word." It wasn't his fault. He was just doing his job, but in a nice way he was giving me time to prepare for what was surely to come.

Suddenly this comfortable job, this position where I thought I might retire, was incredibly unstable. I began to panic as I wondered what I would do and how I would take care of Lavonne and the kids and how we could keep our nice little house. "God, I need your help, again!" I pleaded. Once again, I had given God permission to intervene in our lives and once again, He did.

I soon learned that two of the engineers in our department decided to take early retirement. That placed me at number six. Then another co-worker announced he was going out to start his own business. Now I was number five, but it meant I would still be cut. Then, believe it or not, yet another engineer decided he would relocate. Now I was number four! My job was safe, at least for the moment, and I was able to take a breath and decide what I would do if it ever happened again. Because what I was learning about the aluminum industry was that it would surely happen again.

That thought shook me up. Maybe this wasn't the place where we were to retire. I decided to keep my eyes open for what other opportunities might come when I received a call a year later from the engineer who had left Kaiser to start his own company.

"Rudy, I saw the work you were doing at Kaiser Aluminum, and I'm at a point where I need help programming computers," he began. "Would you be interested in coming to work for me? We're a new company, so I admit there is some risk, but I think there's a good market for what I'm trying to do. I would be able to pay you the same salary as what you are making now."

It was an interesting offer. His company was attempting something that had not been done before which was to completely automate road inspections. In the year he had been gone he had designed on paper a large, fully automated, comprehensive and complex computer system that would use special equipment to inspect roads. This system would collect data that could process the wear and tear on the roads automatically at the push of a button. But it was still all on paper. They were ready to begin implementation of the system and he wanted to bring me on board in a key role to design the software needed to make it happen. Now, all of a sudden my study of microcomputers, programming, CPU's, etc. all came into play. What they were proposing had never been done, and now that I look back, I think he was actually thirty years ahead of his time. It was innovative to say the least.

I discussed the opportunity with Lavonne and my in-laws. Lavonne was hesitant about the change, but her parents were definitely against it. They were concerned that we were leaving the "security" of a larger company, for the unknown future of a start-up. They had a good point, and I even began to question the sanity in considering the offer. But the longer I considered the new position, the more I realized how closely it fit into my dream. If I took the job, I would be able to watch first-hand, the steps in starting a new business. Plus, I would have the opportunity to utilize what I had learned and studied in the area of software, and gain even more understanding while someone else paid me. The more I thought about it, the more I felt it was the right move for us. I was ready to take the position. Lavonne agreed rather hesitantly, but trusted me. So I accepted the offer. I've never backed off from a challenge and this job was certainly that. It was a rewarding, learning experience as it enabled me to write the software that would create something that could work not only on paper, but in real life.

Even as we made this change in my career, there was another more important change that took place in our lives. I refer to it as the hand of God "stirring the pot." He was moving us out of our comfort zone and drawing us to Him. It came in the way of an invitation from friends that had recently moved to Spokane.

"Please join us for church," they invited time and again. Our friends were attending what we referred to as "the church up on the hill." Since moving to Washington, we were in the habit of attending Catholic mass almost every Sunday. Our friends knew I was Catholic. What were they inviting us to church for? I knew the Ten Commandments. I hadn't killed anybody. I was already religious. What was the difference?

Lavonne on the other hand was wide open to their invitation. Recently she had begun to read some small books that a friend had given her from a popular Bible teacher in Tulsa, Oklahoma. "Why don't we give it a try?" she asked. "It can't hurt to visit at least once."

About that same time, there was another event that occurred at Mass that should have alerted me to look closer. One Sunday, Lavonne and I went up to take communion. I was given the elements and turned to go back to my seat. Lavonne was right behind me. What I didn't realize was that when it was her turn, the woman dispensing the elements said to her, "Uh oh, I know you. You're not Catholic. I cannot give you communion."

Emotions swirling, Lavonne turned and walked back to the pew. She didn't mention it until later when I learned how much it had hurt her that she had been turned away from taking communion. After that incident, I encouraged Lavonne to take the courses and steps necessary to become a "legal Catholic" so that she, too, could take communion. Lavonne took the classes, albeit rather hesitantly.

It wasn't long after, that we decided to take our friends up on their invitation to attend "the church up on the hill." If nothing else, it would get them off our backs. But I wasn't prepared for what we found.

As we walked in the door, I was shocked as I scanned the room to take in the scene before me. The music was loud, the people were loud, and the place was rocking. Was this a church or a party? "Wow, what is this?" I asked as I took in the joy that filled the room. The loud worship music, clapping, dancing and raised hands of the congregation was mesmerizing. I had never seen anything like it in a religious service. "What is this all about?" I wondered.

It shook me. It was so very different from the Catholic Church that I didn't know what to do with it. "It's all right. It will be over soon," I told myself. But in reality it wasn't—and I discovered I didn't want it to be. As the pastor stepped into the pulpit, his message seemed directed straight at me. I was mesmerized. There was power in his words and it all made sense, like pieces of a puzzle falling together. Was he really talking about the Bible? I had never heard of some of the things he shared. After the service ended and we got back home I went to grab my Bible. I looked up many of the references he shared to verify what he said. Sure enough, there it was in my very own Bible. How could that be that I didn't know these things?

On Sundays as we left for church we would hit an intersection. If we turned right, it would take us to the Catholic Church and Mass. If we turned left, it would take us to the church up the hill. "What's it going to be?" Lavonne asked each Sunday as we hit the intersection? In reality, that intersection represented our lives. Which direction we were going to turn?

Needless to say, we went back to the church up the hill often. Each time it seemed that the service sped by unlike when we attended mass where I would keep looking at my watch, willing the priest to finish. At the church up the hill, the pastor would speak for as long as an hour and a half at times and never once did I look at my watch. He was filling my soul which had been empty. Lavonne sensed it as well. Something was happening to us as for the first time the Bible came alive and we began to understand.

After every service, I would come back to the house and check out the scriptures the pastor had referenced. Each time I found that he had spoken truthfully. As an engineer it was engrained in me to search for mistakes. I was certain the pastor was going to eventually make one, and I was going to be there when he did. In the meantime, my heart was changing as God drew us to Him and opened our eyes to His truth.

It was near Easter when Lavonne finally finished her classes with the Catholic Church. There was a special two-hour celebration Mass for those who had completed the course culminating in their ability to take

Communion. She felt a sense of relief that from now on no one could prevent her from joining in the communion experience. She was officially a Catholic. The next morning was Easter Sunday.

We had come to that intersection on our drive, when Lavonne turned to me.

"What's it going to be, Rudy?"

"We just attended the long mass yesterday. Would you mind if we go back to the church up the hill?" Lavonne asked.

I gladly agreed. The decision was getting easier and easier.

That Easter Sunday was a day that changed my life.

Close to the end of the service, the pastor gave an invitation to accept Jesus Christ as Lord. As he did I felt a strong desire to go forward. My mind was hesitant, but inside my heart I felt that was what I needed to do. I decided to get out of my chair and go forward. When I reached the front the most amazing thing happened. I looked up and it was as if there was a hole in the sky and I was peering into it as if it were a window giving me a glimpse into heaven. I felt a warm glow inside and I sensed God speaking to my heart, "Son, I love you so much, with no conditions whatsoever. I love you because I created you. You are my son. I have *good* plans for you and your family. You'll always be able to trust me and call me your Father. Never forget that."

How could I? In that moment, I was transformed and completely changed. It was as if a weight had dropped from my shoulders and I felt His presence flood over me like a warm waterfall.

I could not contain my tears of joy. I wept for several minutes as I realized how much God loved me and how much He had done for me. After I went back to my seat, I leaned over and whispered in Lavonne's ear, "I just got born again."

"What?? I just became Catholic!" Lavonne laughed quietly. But the smile on her face said it all. It was a funny, but beautiful moment. The irony was that we had been trying so hard to do the right thing and perform the right rituals to have a good life and in the end it wasn't about any of that. Instead, God showed up, filled us up and let us know that He would take care of us. And as I looked back over my life, I recognized that He had been doing that all along.

Lavonne was happy with my decision to give my heart to the Lord and together we embarked on a new journey. It was unlike anything I had imagined. But that didn't mean it was always a piece of cake. In fact, my life was about to get turned upside down.

Chapter 8

MORE QUESTIONS THAN ANSWERS

Have you ever come to a place in your life when you realize how much you didn't know? That was where I found myself.

From the time I was a child raised in the Catholic Church, I had the sense that God was an old man, sitting in a big seat in the sky ready to punish me for any mistake I made. If I missed a Mass, I felt guilty and had to attend more to make up for it. If I did something wrong, I had to go to the priest to confess the transgression and he would instruct me on the amount of penance I needed to perform to achieve "forgiveness." The problem with that mentality is it paints the picture that God is angry with us; that we have to prove ourselves to receive his love, and that it is all up to what we do. What I was beginning to learn was it wasn't about what I did, but Who He was and how much He loved me.

In order to really understand, I knew I had to start at the beginning, and that meant reading the Bible and learning for myself. *That* wasn't as straight forward as it sounds. Lavonne went to the store and purchased a New International Version Bible that I began to read and study. I usually read about two pages a day so that I can really soak it all in. Of course, at that rate, it took me a long time to read the entire book.

I admit the first time I read through the Bible, very little made sense to me. It was difficult to follow. Can you relate? But I knew it held the key to my life. And like any puzzle, I was determined to find the pieces that fit. In the end, I learned it wasn't that hard, I just had to find a new way of thinking.

The first time I read the Bible it took me about five years! Not because I'm a slow reader, but because I took time with each passage and story. It wasn't a race to finish, but a journey to understanding. At first I had trouble identifying with the people in the stories. I struggled with the mixture of good, evil, deception, rules, animal sacrifices, and introduction of heaven and hell. As I started reading, I had some immediate questions, for example, in Genesis 1:3 it says, *"And God said, 'Let there be light,' and there was light."* It sounds simple and amazing. But where did the light come from? According to the Bible, the sun and the moon were not created until the fourth day. So, it had to be a different kind of light than we know. As I continued to read the Bible, I found other clues such as John 8:12 where Jesus said, *"I am the light of the world. Whoever follows me will never walk in darkness, but will have the light of life."* So was Jesus Himself the light the first day? Another verse from I John 1:5 states, *"God is light; in Him there is no darkness at all."* So maybe it meant that darkness just could not exist while God was present? I didn't know.

Even as I contemplated that question and the issue of light, more questions arose. On the fourth day of creation, God said, "Let there be lights in the vault of the sky to separate the day from the night, and let them serve as signs to mark sacred times, and days and years,"

If that was so, then the actual days—meaning twenty-four hours in a day—marked by the sun did not begin until the fourth day. So what determined the time of day during the first three days of creation? Was Earth turning by itself every twenty-four hours without the sun or was it stationary and not turning at all? Ah! It can be confusing!

There were other places that as I read, the Bible seemed to contradict itself. Or did it?

I read in Genesis 1:12 that during the third day of creation, *"the land produced vegetation: plants bearing seed according to their kinds and trees bearing fruit with seed in it according to their kinds."* Next, I read in Genesis 1:27 that during the sixth day of creation, He created mankind. This was two days after the land produced vegetation.

But then in Genesis 2:4-7, I read that God formed a man from the dust of the ground and breathed into his nostrils the breath of life, and the man became a living being when no shrub had yet appeared on the earth and no plant had yet sprung up.

So which is it? Was vegetation already there or not when man was created?

Again, being an engineer, I'm wired to make sure everything connects and makes sense. I struggle if I don't understand. These kinds of questions can make us confused and tempt us to dismiss the Bible, stop reading it, and blame it on the person who wrote it.

Personally, I don't think God gets frustrated at these questions. I think He welcomes them, because it is an invitation to have a discussion with Him and get to know Him. And God will always honor our desire to get to know Him.

So even though I had more questions than answers, I kept going. When I finished reading the Bible the first time, I started all over again and then again. It was on my third time through that things began to click. I began to understand what God was saying and doing, and in the end I discovered it really wasn't that hard to understand. For it finally dawned on me that from the beginning, when he created Adam and Eve and the beautiful garden for them to live all the way to the story of where He sent His son to the world, He had one goal, one motive. That was to have relationship with us. Crazy right?

The fourth time I read it through, it became obvious to me that God was in love with us, His Creation, and that He wanted only good things for us. That realization helped me to eliminate once and for all, that old image of God sitting in the sky angry at us. He was in fact, in love with us---even when we failed.

Story after story in the Bible became clear as I read it with that underlying message now firmly in place. I began to see where one book of the Bible connected to another. That in each story He wanted us to see that He loved us and was our Creator. That He was there to deliver us from evil and satisfy us during our life journey with peace and hope.

The fifth time I read the Bible---has been the best yet. This journey has taken me twenty-five years and each time with more understanding, that God is not only our Father, but our friend. He wants not just a simple relationship with us, but a deep relationship in which we come to Him and trust Him with everything we have and everything we are. It has made me feel as if I am His favorite son. In the second part of this book, I wrote a summary just for you of what I have read and studied all these years. I want you to see that God is in love with His creation and that includes you. Whether you know it or not and whether you like it or not, He loves you and wants a deeper relationship with you.

That relationship I was developing with Him gave me a deep inner peace that I cannot describe, which was good, because there were unsettled times looming on our horizon.

Chapter 9

WE CAN'T PAY YOU ANYMORE

As we experienced this new life, so did our family as we welcomed our third child, Daniel (Danny) into the world. The girls were now three and five and it didn't seem life could get much better.

We continued to attend the church up on the hill and as I grew in my knowledge and relationship with God, I realized I had somewhere to go with all my questions regarding my future. I no longer felt I was alone trying to figure out what I would do with my life and career. It was such a relief

Day by day, I could sense His leading and speaking to my heart as I read the Bible and prayed. That may sound strange to you if you have never experienced it. But trust me when I say it is real, and it is available to anyone who desires that type of relationship with God.

As I prayed, He impressed on my heart that I was at the right place, at the right time, doing the right thing---exactly what he had prepared me to do. As I stated before, each of us are created with gifts and talents for a destiny. So, even as God was giving me peace that I was at the right job, I still had this desire for my own business. Where did that come from and what was I to do with that? He lovingly assured me that He had created that in my heart and that my position in this new start-up business, was exactly where he wanted me—at least for now.

I was learning to trust Him with the details—and the timing.

Lavonne and I were growing by leaps and bounds in our knowledge of the Bible and of God. The more we read the Bible, the more insight and wisdom we had, not just of who He is, but of what He wanted for our lives. I remember as we sat in church and our pastor made the statement about "living by faith." I didn't really even know what that meant, so I asked Him one day. "Lord, I keep hearing this thing about living by faith. I don't know what that means. Can you show me what it means to live by faith?" Never doubt that God hears your prayers. I know He heard that one, and what happened next was complete proof.

The next thing I knew I had this desire, this intense desire, to be a blessing to other people. I was getting a clear and strong revelation that He was blessing us, so that we could be a blessing to others. He uses us to be an extension of Himself—to be generous, loving, compassionate and merciful. Lavonne and I discussed it at length, and in the end determined that we would take part of my income to help the poor in our community.

I remember clearly wrestling with God on that issue. In our minds we often tend to think that if we give something away, we may need it later. It goes against our nature, our flesh, to operate that way and fear can try to take over. Yet God heard my prayer about wanting to know what it meant to live by faith. He was beginning to open my eyes to the concept of sowing and reaping, and how to be a blessing to others. I understood the concept of tithing (giving ten percent) and we were doing that, but I wanted more. I wanted to *really* be a blessing to others.

We started to become aware of those in need in our community. When we gave to help them, it would fill us with such joy. It was an incredible thing. They were getting blessed by the gift, but we were getting blessed because we gave. I started thinking more seriously about how to be a blessing to others.

I have to be honest with you. In my head I did not want to further touch my salary to increase our giving. We already put aside a portion of my salary to give away. We had our budget and it was working okay. We had to watch closely every dollar we spent, but our basic needs were being met.

Since I did not want to further touch my regular pay, I decided to make an offer to God. "God, I want to be a blessing to others. So I promise I will give away half of any extra income I make." *So what about that God?* I thought to myself.

To me it was the safest route possible to start learning about living by faith, how to be a blessing to others and how to make a covenant with God. And I did not have to change our regular budget which I thought was providing for us.

It wasn't that I was out looking for extra jobs, but they just seemed to find me after we made that pledge to the Lord. Not long after, I got a call from a friend. "Hey Rudy, I know you're a computer programmer. Can you write this little program for me? I can pay you $100 to do the job." The job was a piece of cake for me. All of a sudden I had an extra $50 for my family and $50 I could give away. "Okay God," I said. "Thanks for the extra money. Who do you want me to give the extra $50 to?" Inevitably, a need in the community would arise right before our eyes.

Then, the jobs started pouring in. The thing was, I wasn't out looking for the work!

The more money we gave away, the easier it became and the "security blanket" of money had less and less of a hold on me. The funny thing was, even as the jobs kept pouring in, so did our awareness of needs around us. Sometimes we would be out shopping and bump into a friend that had a need, or run into an acquaintance that had a financial need. Each time the money was there that we could help them out and it filled us with joy. Looking back, I recognize that God was preparing us. He was showing us how He worked to provide and He was also preparing us for bigger things. I thought this is what it meant to live by faith. I was about to learn there was more.

As I mentioned, the new company I worked for was ambitious and innovative in their concept to design a program that would fully automate road inspections. The process at that time was that an individual would go out on the shoulder of the roads with pen and paper in hand and manually record the problems on the road and how many repairs were needed. This process was both unsafe and highly speculative. There was no consistency to the reports.

My new employer had an idea that would fully automate the process. The only problem I discovered as I began to work on the automated system, was that the computers and video technology in existence at that time weren't fast enough or capable enough to accomplish the task.

"Listen, this is a monster of a thing you guys want to develop," I told them. "Our computers aren't fast enough or have enough space to accomplish the task. It's too complex. It's a great idea, but I think we need to simplify it." I truly believed the market would still greatly benefit from a simplified version of what he wanted. But my boss wouldn't hear of it, so we kept marching ahead on the same path. The only problem is their money had run out.

The week before Christmas I got called into the office. Somehow I knew it wasn't because I was about to get a Christmas bonus.

"Rudy, we like you a lot and we like the work you do, but we've come to the point where we don't have enough money to continue to pay your salary. If you want to stay, that's fine. We have some contracts that are pending and when they go through, you will be the first one to be paid. However, until that time we can no longer pay you a salary."

Now Lavonne and I got to see the other side of "living by faith." But it also meant we got to see God in action.

I immediately started to look for another position. That just made sense. Unfortunately, there weren't any openings. I contacted friends and people I knew in the industry. Nothing. I started really "shaking the bushes." Still nothing. That's when desperation started to set it. I hadn't brought home a check in several weeks now and on top of that, Lavonne was pregnant with our fourth child. What were we going to do?

The Lord reminded me of the time back to in my childhood when He had provided for me in a miraculous way. That was way before I really knew Him, and yet I wanted to believe there was a God and so I prayed to Him. As I mentioned, my parents rarely had any extra money for non-essential items. So if we wanted to do something or buy something, we had to figure out a way to earn the money. I remember it was a very hot summer day when I saw my three brothers getting ready to go somewhere. "Where are you going?" I asked. "Swimming!" they responded. I wanted to go with them, but there was an entrance fee of one colón (the Costa Rican currency) to swim and I didn't even have a cent. My brothers had all earned some money and so prepared to go to the public pool.

"Can you loan me one colón so I can go with you?" I asked them, but each in turn shook their head. They only had enough for themselves. I was devastated. I wanted to go with them so badly. I asked both Mom and Dad. I remember the sadness in my mother's eyes as she let me know she had no money to give me.

I ran out of the house bawling my eyes out. Life was so unfair. I walked down the street and sat down on the curb with my head in my hands as I continued my cry-fest. I wanted to go so badly. "God, I really, really, really want to go swimming with my brothers," I said through my tears.

Eventually the sobs stopped and my heart calmed. As I looked up I noticed something glimmering in the sun in the middle of the gravel road. I dashed over to the spot. Laying on the ground was a one colón coin. Immediately I bent down and picked it up stuffing it into my pants. To have that kind of money in my pocket made me feel like a millionaire. It was a miracle! I was just about to run back to the house and tell my brothers I could go with them, when all of a sudden I had another thought. The other day I had seen some candy in the store. It looked amazing. With the colón now burning a hole in my pocket, I wondered how much candy I could purchase with it and what it would taste like. So I turned around and started walking towards the "pulperia" or local grocery store. In the end I didn't even use the money for the purpose I had prayed, and yet God had graciously provided for me in an undeniably supernatural way.

I continued to ponder and pray over our dilemma. Since there were no job openings that I could find, I chose to stay where I was and keep working at my present job, by faith, trusting that when they got paid on a contract, so would I. In the meantime, I continued to get calls from friends for those extra side jobs. The thing was that although this really was "extra" income right now, but it was our *only* income. I had promised God we would give away fifty percent of our *extra* income. Did that still count now that our situation had changed?

"You made a promise," Lavonne reminded me as we discussed the situation one night. "I think we should keep it." It was really hard, but I recognized she was right and decided to keep the promise I had made.

That's when we really started living by faith---and seeing miracles. It was exciting and scary all at the same time.

Jobs were coming in from all over for me to work on computers of friends and acquaintances. $100 here and $200 there. But I could only count on half of that as *my* income. It was incredible to watch. We learned during that season that we needed to be specific with our prayers. One week we needed $100 in food, plus a new pair of shoes as well as $50 for something else for the kids. We prayed and trusted God to provide. Sure enough, an extra job came that week that provided double the amount of our own needs. So, we were able to take care of our family and still give away half to someone else.

I remember clearly one week when we needed $150. No extra jobs had come in for several days. All we knew to do was to continue to pray and trust God. Later that day, I went to the mailbox and inside was a letter from the student credit union of Oregon State University. "Dear Rodolfo, you left your account open when you left the school and it has not been used for several years. We need to close it. What would you like to us to do with the funds?"

What? That had been seven years ago. I had lived in two different places in Costa Rica and moved from Portland to Spokane during that time. I have no idea how they tracked me down, but the timing couldn't have been better.

I called them immediately, "Please send us whatever money is in the account to me as soon as possible," I informed the clerk. I looked at Lavonne as I hung up the phone as a smile spread across my face. It was unbelievable.

Two days later, the check arrived in the mail. $305. It was what we needed for that week to pay our bills, plus the half we needed to give away. That is when I realized and understood what it was to live by faith.

As we continued to give to others, God continued to give to us. It reminded me of one of the stories I had read in the Bible where Jesus took five loaves of bread and two fish—a small lunch from a small boy—prayed over it, and then divided it until it fed over five thousand people[1]. It was impossible, and yet we were learning that God could do the same miracles now.

"This is how I work, Rudy. I'm here. I love you and I will provide for you."

It was awesome.

About that time, my mother came to Spokane to visit us. It was her first time in the States in a while as she and my family had not been able to attend our wedding in the States. It was wonderful having her in our home and for our kids to have time with their Costa Rican grandmother. It stirred up so many good memories for me as I watched her play with our kids. It also stirred another memory. That's when I got a new idea for a business.

"Mom, do you remember how to make "roscas"? I asked one day?

Roscas were delicious crunchy sweet treats mom used to make when we had the money available for her to buy the ingredients. Shaped like a small pretzel she would mix the batter, roll them out and bake them. The house filled with their aroma and my mouth would be watering before they ever came out of the oven. They were a huge hit with all my siblings as well.

"Can you make a batch now, Mom? Do it slowly so I can write down the ingredients, measurements and all the steps, please." Mom actually had to make several batches before I got it written down correctly, but before she left to return to Costa Rica a couple of weeks later, I was able to make the delectable treat just like she did.

We launched the Sonrise Food snack business not long afterwards. I renamed the roscas "bread chips" and changed the pretzel shape to a flat cracker to simplify the production process. I also designed tools so that we could begin a small-scale mass production of the chips that I was convinced would change the world. It seemed that my desire for my own business was finally taking off!

About that same time, Lavonne and I were attending a small group in our church. The leader was teaching about the importance of writing down our vision and keeping it before us. That really resonated with me. A few days later after I got off work, I took a piece of paper and went to a quiet place. I did some real soul searching. What was the vision inside me?

As I sat before the Lord and prayed He began to burn these thoughts within me and it began to pour out almost without thought. I went to the computer and began to type the following:

SONRISE FOODS BUSINESS VISION OF RUDY BLANCO – 1989

This is a company founded in the inspiration of being an example of God's plans for His people. We want Jesus Christ to be our partner and we want Him, through the Holy Spirit, to have a major role in the decision-making process of every minor and major decision. We want Him to direct this company and to guide it according to God's perfect plans. We want to reach and touch people with the love of God; people inside the company and people outside the company.

Inside the company, we desire the peace and joy of God to be present in every place and that it will be manifested in the persons working in this company. There will always be something special in the atmosphere that every person will experience. The work that is done in every workplace will be something that each worker will enjoy and will always look forward to do. The satisfaction of each task completed will be credited to the help that we receive from the Holy Spirit.

We will always be proud of the products we produce, because we put our best effort into making them. We will always look for better ways of making them and or better quality for our customers. We honor what we do, because we do our best. We are open to suggestions for change. We are open, because we know that these suggestions are honest and well-intended. Everybody puts the well-being of the company in high priority, because the well-being of the company means the well-being of every person in it. We want to always be united and we want to always experience the power behind the unity of people with common goals.

With God, anything is possible. We pray for the Spirit of Peace to be with us always. We all are against negative criticism, talking behind other people's backs, and lack of communication. We all realize that we are spending a great deal of time together and we are determined to make the best out of it. We are willing to work out any differences by communicating our feelings and thoughts to the other people. There will always be a good level of communication between every member of this company.

We are against waste. Waste of time. Waste of materials. Waste of talents. Waste of opportunities. We believe that every person should be doing the work that best fits his/her abilities and desires. We want the work that we do here to provide the same satisfaction that doing hobbies does. We believe that every person is responsible for the quality of the functions they share of the company. The first responsibility falls on the company to provide necessary training programs and communication skills so every person is aware of how their work affects the performance of other people in the process.

The company recognizes that the best asset a company can have is its people—motivated people willing to share the same vision and goals of the company. In the same way, the rewards will be high and above the normal standards.

Outside the company, we want to share the good news of our success, which is based on making God our partner in the name of Jesus Christ. We are excited about telling other people that God lives with us and that God works with us, and that the same success waits for anybody that puts his/her trust in God and makes Him an important part of his/her life.

We will also reach other people by honoring God with fifty percent of our profits. Those resources are to be used according to the direction of the Holy Spirit on areas that have to deal with spreading the gospel to less fortunate children and young people, so they can know and experience God and His love, and maintain a close relationship with Jesus Christ.

The bread chip business didn't make it. While it might have been easy to look at that and become discouraged, something more powerful did survive from that experience and that was the business vision and model I received that night from the Lord. Kind of like the company I was working for, it was just a little ahead of its time. As the business closed, I tucked this manifesto away for safe keeping.

It turns out I was going to need it.

Chapter 10

THE PILLAR IS MOVING

L ife is full of transitions. The choices we make during those transitions and opportunities set the course for the next season in our lives. This can be seen from a story in the Bible in the book of Exodus. It showed how the Israelites walked through a miraculous transition from slavery to freedom.

The Israelite leader, Moses, was leading over a million Jews out of Egypt—a land of slavery for them—to a land God had promised them[2]. The impossibility of that scenario never ceases to amaze me. Moses had a million people, men, women, and children depending on him. They were in the middle of the desert and yet they needed food and water--for a million people! I'm sure there were times he had to ask God, "What were you thinking?"

At times, I wanted to ask God that same question as I continued to work at my old job with no paycheck--and I had only myself, my wife and my three kids to take care of! Our needs were being provided for, but let me just say that "living by faith" takes faith, and it wasn't always easy.

If you read further into the story of Moses and the Israelites, it's clear it wasn't really Moses leading, but God. We learn that there, in the desert, He provided His Presence that remained with them in the form of a pillar of cloud by day and a pillar of fire by night. It protected them. It guided them[3]. It says (when the pillar moved, they moved. If it stayed they stayed.[4]) They didn't make the decision to move on their own. They were living by faith and allowed Him to guide them. That was where Lavonne and I found ourselves: waiting on God to see what He would do. That's when our "pillar" began to move. The question was, were we going to move with it?

I received a call from a civil engineer in Norman, Oklahoma. He was the brother of a friend, of a friend. My friend had told him about me after he learned of this man's desire to start a company very similar to the one for which I had been working—a company that would specialize in road inspection equipment and services. Now as he introduced himself over the phone, he told me about the company he wanted to start. I was immediately intrigued.

"Rudy, I want to build a business that provides some sort of automated road inspection services, and I've heard you have extensive experience in this field. Do you know what to do to make that happen?"

I broke out in a smile as I listened to his dream for his company. "I know exactly what to do…exactly," I replied without hesitation.

"Will you consider moving to Oklahoma and to help me launch this new company?" he asked.

Several more conversations occurred before I took the position where he outlined his desire and my compensation. In essence, he would provide the finances and I would provide the know-how. We agreed to a financial package in which he would own fifty-two percent of the company and I would get twenty-four percent and he was to reserve another twenty-four percent for another partner in the future. The company would be split into two areas: data collection in the field and data processing in the office.

Lavonne was now pregnant with our fourth child and neither she nor I wanted to leave our friends or church family, but we both sensed that the job in Norman was our next step. I immediately had peace. I sensed God speak to me that Oklahoma was going to be our Promise Land. We put our house up for sale and after just two days we received an offer. We accepted it, packed our things, loaded the kids in the car, and said good-bye to our cute little house. One chapter in our lives was closing, but another was opening and I wondered if with it, I would finally realize my dream for my own business.

My first day on the job, I met my new boss and partner. We shook hands. He walked me through the warehouse, as he did talking and sharing his ideas. It was exhilarating to think that my dream of company ownership was coming true. Even though the company wasn't all mine. I had a stake in it and that was rewarding. "I know what to do," I assured him as he walked me through the office and showed me where I would work. I was completely confident that I could do the job, bringing with me the technical knowledge and expertise of what I had learned from my previous position plus my own idea of what I felt could work. His desire was to create a company that could provide road inspection services. I knew I could do it, and immediately knew what tools we needed and where to start to build a simple, partly manual, partly automated, road inspection system.

Our family kept growing as our fourth child, Mark was born in September of that year. This kept Lavonne as busy at home as I was at the office.

Within two years, I had developed a vehicle system to collect data in the field that was well-received in the industry. The new system sold well, and the company was profitable. With the success of the company, was my own growing success, as I made a name for myself in this specialized field. I got to know the leaders, end-users and engineers in the road and transportation world. Lavonne and I continued to give away part of our income to those in need as had been our practice in Spokane. That was never going to change, and we sensed God's pleasure as we reached out to bless others with the things in which He had blessed us.

It was satisfying work and I remember, just as in my first job with Kaiser Aluminum, that sense of contentment. That same feeling that maybe this would be the place that we would retire crept into my thinking. After all, I had a share in this company, so it was like having my own business and filled that desire at least to a certain degree. I was making pretty much all the technical decisions, which was rewarding. My boss made all the management and financial decisions which left me to do the creative side. That was the perfect set up as far as I was concerned.

I'm not sure why it took me so long, but about two years into the job and after we began selling the systems I had created, I started to wonder why I had never seen any profits from my twenty-four percent of the company. I finally went to my boss. My salary had remained the same in spite of the additional income that was coming in through the sales.

"The system has been selling well. But I haven't seen any of the profit sharing as we discussed in my contract. What's up?" I asked. I remember I didn't like his answer which was evasive at best. I continued to bring the topic up when I was around him and each time I felt I got the run around as to why I hadn't seen any profits personally. I knew he had taken several vacation trips and had even done some international travel with his wife. I knew how many systems we had sold and that we were doing well. Something didn't make sense.

I continued to press the issue until one day he responded, "Rudy, I want to give you your twenty-four percent of the company, but you're going to have to pay for it," he responded finally.

What? Pay for something that was already supposed to be part of my payment? That didn't make sense. Had I really heard right?

Puzzled I tried to get clarification. "What do you mean, pay for it?" I asked. "When we started the company, we agreed that I would receive

86

twenty-four percent of the company and now you're saying I have to buy my way in?"

My boss started throwing around numbers, which didn't make sense, and only brought more confusion to the conversation. It was obvious he didn't want to honor his agreement now that I had the system completed. I looked at him, my mind swirling as I tried to process this shift. Sensing I wasn't going to leave without a resolution, he finally responded, "Okay, I'll give you twenty-four percent of the company. We can arrange for you to begin to receive a small percentage of profits, but then you will have to apply those to immediate payment of the twenty-four percent of the company you are going to receive."

I looked at him and wanted to laugh at the contradiction within his own statement. How could you "give me" part of the company, and then turn around and require me to pay for it? My boss continued to talk in circles using financial terms like interest, multiplication of the initial investment, the rate of return, etc. These were terms I didn't completely understand at the time, but it didn't matter. What I did know was that we had a serious problem. Since the beginning, he had paid me a straight salary, like a regular employee, rather than a part owner in the company. From my perspective, he wasn't honoring what he had promised.

My boss's personal expenditures on big ticket items continued. It was hard to watch him benefit extensively from the profit of the company and still refuse to honor his original commitment to me and my share of the company. Finally, I confronted him on the issue, "From now on, I'm going to add up how much you spend on personal items and trips and I insist that I receive twenty-four percent of that amount." I knew it wasn't a full twenty-four percent of the profits I should have received, but without access to the books, I had no other way to monitor profits. My boss agreed, at least for a while, to my demand and for at least a couple of years I received extra income. Until one day, he walked in my office with some paperwork.

"Rudy, my lawyer drew up this contract which I would like you to sign stating your twenty-four percent ownership in the company."

Finally, it looked like he was going to do the right thing. But as I scanned the document, I discovered that although it was better, it required I pay him several hundred thousand dollars for that ownership. I shook my head. That was never going to happen.

Our relationship began to deteriorate from there when he made another business decision that I questioned. Up to that point, I had basically been running the company. My boss knew nothing about software, programming or computers. He left all of that to me. But one day, he announced he was bringing his son in to help run the business. In reality, he turned over almost everything to his son. Almost immediately, the quality of the data and content we were shipping to our customers changed. It got sloppy and I began to receive calls from frustrated customers. "Rudy, we didn't get the kind of data we requested. This stuff is no good. What are you going to do about it?"

The problem was that although my boss was the majority owner in the company, people in the industry had been working with me as the creator of the system. It was my name that was associated with the company and the data, and now what we were sending out wasn't meeting the high standards as before as his son continued to take over and make the shots.

I went to my boss and voiced my concerns. It was obvious, at least to me, that his son didn't have the necessary experience to run the company successfully, but my concerns fell on deaf ears. Our relationship became even more difficult and friction filled the air as I continued to fight for quality control for our customers. As my boss and I continued to talk, I realized he had a completely different vision for the company than my own. He had the mind of a civil engineer and liked surveys and detailed data. He wanted to apply the resources and energy of the company predominantly to inspecting airports and bridges. He felt that held the greatest potential for the company. I completely disagreed. I felt we should focus on the pavement management needs of the government transportation departments across the country.

We had another serious issue facing the company as well. The software industry was changing. We were still using an old DOS computer operating system, which was all that was available when we had started a few years before. It wasn't user-friendly and it lacked the ability to insert graphics. Since that time Microsoft had launched their new Windows software. It was innovative, but the program had issues. That is until the release of Windows '95. That was a game-changer. I knew for our company to be able to continue to compete in the market place, I would have to rewrite all the programs using Windows '95 as our old DOS system would no longer be adequate. It was a daunting project, but necessary. Yet, he and I were in complete disagreement as to how the company should move forward.

As the situation continued to spiral out of control, I recognized that this was *not* going to be the company from which I retired. It was clear the "pillar of cloud" was moving and I was going to move with it.

Chapter 11

FREEZING MY TOES OFF TO BIRTH A VISION

I was working at my desk one day when my boss's son walked in with some paperwork. He laid it in front of me. He began to talk as I scanned the document. It was a non-compete agreement, which he was giving to all the employees to sign. After he left, I looked over the document in detail. "Perhaps this is my ticket to finally get my twenty-four percent of the company," I thought to myself. I laid the document in a pile on my desk unsigned. When the son comes back for it, I thought I would let him know I would sign it if they would keep to their agreement to give me the twenty-four percent of the company which I had been promised--without requiring financial outlay on my part. Weeks passed, but he never came back. Lavonne and I continued to pray for direction. Something had to give.

One day, as I was in the son's office looking for something, I noticed a note on his desk from the company attorney that read, "We have all the employee's signed non-compete agreements except Rudy's. Why don't you try to get him to sign it and send it to me?"

I waited for him to come and ask me for the agreement, certain that it would be any day, but still he didn't.

Then one morning after I woke, I was flooded by a sense that it was the time for change. I heard God speak to my heart as clearly as if it was an audible voice as He said to me, "This is your time. Get out of the company. I just put a new "baby" inside of you. You're going to give birth to a new company." That was it. I just knew this was His direction and that God was showing me a new path. I was filled with peace.

I met with my boss and his son and turned in my resignation. Almost in unison they cautioned me, "Don't even think about starting another company."

"I never signed the non-compete agreement," I reminded them. There was nothing to prevent me from launching my own company. After all, all the ideas they were working from were mine, and they had never paid me for my ownership in the company. I was completely free to walk away.

But they weren't happy at all with my decision.

My immediate dilemma was the start-up money needed to launch my own company. I received an $8,000 severance package when I left, but it was nowhere close to the $200,000 I needed to launch my new business. I didn't know how Lavonne and I were going to do it. The odds were certainly against us, but I knew God was in control and by now, I knew what it was to live by faith.

When I had prayed for God to teach me what it meant to walk by faith, He took me seriously. I wouldn't change that for anything. Had we not walked by faith, with no money coming in during those years in Spokane, we might not have been willing or able to step out now in this new adventure with no steady paycheck. But we had already seen God provide for our family in supernatural ways. We knew, without a doubt, that He would continue to do just that.

Just one month shy of the ten-year deadline I had given God to "do something with my life," and help me start my own business, I walked into the government offices in Oklahoma City and filed the necessary paperwork to start on this new path that God was showing to us. In keeping with that, I named the company Pathway Services Inc.

Lavonne and I had been married sixteen years by this time, now with four small children living in Norman. A few years before, Lavonne had made the decision to homeschool our kids. She had her hands full with that important job, and was unable to assist with the company as I set up a work area in the basement of our home. It was a no-frills basic work space. In that area I had only a bed, a desk, a computer and an excitement I'd never experienced before.

We invested $600 immediately to purchase Windows '95 and a compiler. I already had a personal computer to develop my new system. I went to work there in my small office, writing code and creating a brand-new system for automated road inspections utilizing the new Windows program that allowed for much more flexibility and graphics than I had been able to create in the previous DOS system. The months sped by as I worked and the ideas began to flow. I wanted to create a system that would work with maximum efficiency, from the ground up. This was the third time I had written this type of system and now since technology and computers had improved exponentially from those early days, the program I was writing could do so much more than the previous ones I had written. It took five months to have the initial layout of the first prototype and another four afterwards to bring it to completion and a place that I could move out into a regular office space. God later revealed to me that the nine-month period in that basement was like a "womb" in which I was birthing Pathway Services. When they were done, I had a brand new, semi-automated system that I could use and sell.

Eager to show people the new product that I was developing, I called some connections I had made in Minnesota and North Dakota. An appointment was set for me to come to their offices and demonstrate the system. The only problem was Lavonne and I only had one vehicle, a 1988 manual transmission, Colt Vista. It meant I would have to leave Lavonne and the kids without a vehicle during my absence. It was also the dead of winter. That posed another problem for Lavonne and I both as it made it almost impossible for her to be able to get out and walk anywhere nearby to purchase something if she needed it, and it meant that I was at the mercy of the unpredictable northern climate as I traveled. We prayed and felt I was to go, and so I forged ahead with the planning of the trip to be gone as short of a time as possible. The trip required a lot of driving. As I mapped it out on paper, I would need to drive almost 800 miles the first day, approximately twelve hours, to my first meeting in St. Paul. Immediately after I made the presentation, I would jump back in the car. The next meeting was approximately 400 miles away in Bismarck, North Dakota for a meeting that would take place the following day. We figured if all went as planned, I could make the trip there and back in five days.

The week before the trip, we had just finished the Wednesday night service at church. As we all piled into the car to head home, I discovered the car wouldn't start. I tried the engine so many times that eventually I ran the battery dead. A mechanic in our church, seeing our dilemma, invited me to have the car towed to his shop and he would look at it. We arranged for Lavonne and the kids to get a ride home with another family. Now I just had to get the car towed. We didn't have a rope or chain available to tow the vehicle. In the end, a friend got behind my car with his truck and pushed while I sat in the Colt and steered. Thankfully, the mechanics shop wasn't too far from the church.

I got a call from the mechanic the next day. "Rudy, there is a leak in your heater hose which rusted some wires and prevented the engine from starting. You have two options. The first is I can replace the parts and get it completely fixed. I will need to order the parts to get started." This option was expensive and was going to take several days to complete as we waited for parts. The second option wasn't going to fix the problem, but we could override it so that the car would run. It involved cutting and capping the heater hose to stop the leak. It was an inexpensive option. The only problem was it meant the heater wouldn't work. Because we were already tight on funds, I chose the second option. "How bad can it be?" I thought to myself. I had no idea what I was about to get myself into.

Lavonne wasn't very happy with the decision. "Rudy, you are going up north. You've got to have heat in the car," she admonished when I told her of my decision. I smiled as I tried to put her mind to rest. "I'll be fine," I insisted. Since I had never been in that kind of situation before, I had no idea just how hard it was going to be. In my mind, I thought I could just take a couple of extra blankets and have them in the car with me in case I got too cold.

Tuesday, the day of the trip came and I left for St. Paul early in the morning. The weather was fine, and I didn't miss the lack of heat at first, but somewhere after I hit Kansas, just four to five hours into the trip, it started to get cold. I pulled over and grabbed one of the two blankets and wrapped it around my legs. As long as the blanket remained tight around my legs, I was fine. The problem was, that was impossible since I was driving a manual transmission. Each time I had to move my leg to shift gears, the cold air would swoosh up under the blanket. It finally got so cold that I had to add the second blanket. I finally made it to the hotel in St. Paul. My legs felt like ice as I tried to pull myself out of the car and check in. I welcomed the warmth of the hotel room and the chance to thaw out.

The next morning as I got out to head to my first appointment, the temperatures were frigid and well below freezing. The old Colt Vista, however, started right up and I made it to the appointment and gave my first presentation on the new system I was working on. I could tell the product was well received and I left full of excitement. I hoped the next presentation would go as well as the first.

I shook hands with the pavement management engineers I met with, and put my materials in the back of the Colt and started off toward North Dakota to at least get a few miles in before nightfall. I was just thirty minutes into the trip when the needle on the heat gauge began to point toward hot. When I was on a level plain or going downhill the needle would go back down slightly, but then when I would hit any type of incline, the needle rose significantly indicating my engine was overheating. A few miles later, the engine started to jerk slightly as if it was running out of fuel. I knew I needed to get off the highway as soon as possible to avoid getting stuck out in the middle of nowhere in really cold weather.

I took the next exit. Just as I turned onto the ramp, my engine stopped. I shifted the car into neutral and let the Colt roll. Fortunately, it had enough momentum to glide into the parking lot of a hotel just off the exit. I rolled into a parking spot and stopped. It was already eight or nine p.m. I was cold and tired. I grabbed my bag, and checked into the hotel for the night, ready to be warm. I would deal with the car in the morning.

It was early the next day when I ventured back out to the Colt to assess my situation. I put my key in the ignition. Click. Click. Click. The battery was dead. That was when I noticed a greenish colored liquid under the front part of the car. I popped the hood and twisted off the radiator cap. It was empty. Now what? I walked back to my hotel room to warm up and find a phone book. I started calling mechanics in the area until I found one who could look at the car right away. Now I had to figure out how to get the car to him.

The thought hit me that I first needed to fill the radiator with water. I took the ice bucket from the hotel room and filled it with hot water. I took several trips back and forth to the car until the radiator tank was full. Next, I had to get someone to help me jump the battery. I finally found someone with a truck and jumper cables. As we connected the cables to my battery I prayed that it would start. It did on the first try! I thanked my benefactor and then raced to the mechanic's shop. Afraid that the battery might not hold a charge, I left the car running and ran inside to talk with the mechanic. Unfortunately, since I had called earlier that morning, they had gotten slammed with business. Not only would they not be able to get on it immediately, but I was told I would have to leave the car and they would get to it the next day.

"But I have a business meeting in Bismarck," I said to the mechanic hoping that somehow he could move my car up the list.

"I'm sorry, but I can't get to your car any sooner. But if your temperature gauge remained steady as you drove here, then I recommend buying some coolant to finish filling the radiator tank and then see if it leaks out or not. If the leak has stopped, then you may be fine with driving to Bismarck and getting it fixed there," he explained.

I had to keep my appointment the next day and needed to get back on the road. I did as the mechanic suggested and purchased the coolant. I was hesitant to turn the motor off, afraid it might not start back up, but needed to in order to pour in the liquid. I filled the radiator tank up the remainder of the way with coolant, screwed the cap back on and got back in the car to try the engine. It started right up. Now I just needed to let it run and see if the radiator would hold the coolant. I left it running for quite some time and no leaks appeared. That was a good sign. I made the decision to go back to the hotel, check out, and get back on the road.

Once back on the highway, I kept shifting my vision back to the heat gauge. So far so good, but another issue started to consume my attention. Fog had started to build up on the windshield. It was more than just watery condensation. This was thicker and even after I wiped it away, it almost immediately returned, obstructing my vision. Soon, the fog on the windshield had become so thick that only a small patch could be cleared to see the road ahead. I continued to try the defrost, but it only made conditions worse. No matter what I did, the fog increased. My legs and hands were freezing as I gripped the steering wheel trying to peer out of the small hole where I repeatedly worked to rub away the fog/condensation. My vigil was relentless as I wiped the windshield in front of me and then the window beside me so I could have some side view of the road and traffic. The situation was growing dangerous as every breath I exhaled fogged the window more until I was forced to hold my breath as long as I could. When I could hold it no longer, I finally turned my head to the side and emptied my lungs all while I kept the corner of my eyes still focused on the road ahead.

The bitter cold seeped into every inch of my body. The entire journey became a battle. First to keep the blankets wrapped tightly around my legs, then taking turns wiping areas on the windshield and my side window, so that I could see the road and any other traffic and then turning my head sideways to exhale and avoid fogging the windshield further. I put my foot on the gas pedal. I needed to get to Bismarck and be done with this leg of journey as soon as possible. I was flying down the highway, wiping, wrapping blankets and exhaling to the side. I had just gone over a bridge when I caught a small glimpse of a car parked on the shoulder of the road. My eyes shot down to my speedometer. Ninety mph. Uh oh.

The next thing I knew red and blue lights were flashing in my foggy rearview mirror. My mind immediately flew to our tight financial situation. I really didn't need a ticket right now. But then I thought, "Maybe this is a good thing. I can sit in the police car to warm up as he writes me a ticket and if I did break down, he would be nearby." That was my thought at least.

I pulled over onto the shoulder of the road. As the officer approached my car, I tried to locate my wallet. The heavy blankets wrapped tightly around my legs hindered my movements making it difficult to maneuver and locate my wallet. I finally found it and rolled down my window to talk with the officer.

"May I have your driver's license and proof of insurance," he asked all business like.

I tried to explain my dilemma, but he wasn't interested. He was only interested in writing the ticket, which he then ripped off his pad and handed to me as I shivered in my car. "Slow it down next time," he stated as he walked back to his cruiser.

I pulled back out onto the highway, this time monitoring my speed as well as my ability to see out the windshield. I finally pulled into Bismarck later that afternoon, convinced I was a human ice cube. The good news was the radiator hadn't leaked further, and I thought the battery would be fully recharged after such a long trip. I checked into the hotel room and allowed the warmth of the room to penetrate my cold body. It took a couple of hours before I felt like my body temperature returned to normal!

I set the alarm for a little earlier than needed to have extra time in case the Colt wouldn't start. The next morning as I headed out into the frigid temperatures I shoved my hands in my pockets and forged ahead. I was ready to be done with the cold. I put the key in the ignition and nothing happened.

"Oh, no! I need to get help to start this Colt again!" I thought to myself as my mind whirred into motion accessing what I needed to do. I turned and walked back to the hotel lobby to talk with the desk clerk, "Does anyone have any jumper cables to help me so I can get my car started," I asked him trying to stay calm as I looked at my watch. There was still time to do this. I was thankful I had set my alarm for earlier than needed.

The clerk shook his head and explained what those who live in the harsh northern climate already know. Another car would not be able to get my car started because the temperature was too low and it would not be able to generate enough power. It would require a truck with a generator to have the current needed to get the Colt's engine to fire back up. He provided names of two or three businesses who offered that service, and I immediately started calling. A few minutes later, a truck with a generator showed up. After the tech connected his cables from the generator to the Colt's battery, I sat back down in the driver's seat and turned the key.

I heard a horrible grinding sound of metal against metal as the frozen motor tried to start. I learned an important fact on that trip. Cars in the north were built with a block heater to protect them during the frigid winter temperatures. Many businesses have electrical outlet meters available in the parking lots to plug cars into so it keeps the engine block warm. My little Colt Vista from the south obviously was not equipped with that feature. Even after a four or five-hour drive, the battery had not held a charge. My Colt finally started after a few tries, and I left it running as I checked out and then headed for my meeting.

The meeting went very well, but wasn't over until late afternoon. I knew that after sitting in the cold for several hours the Colt wasn't going to start for me. I was right. So, one of the engineers from the meeting offered to help and followed me out with a huge battery on a dolly. He helped me jump start the Colt and I was on my way once again, this time turning my car toward home.

I planned to drive three hours that first night to stop in Fargo, North Dakota. Although it was only three hours to that destination, within the first hour my feet were so numb with cold I knew I had to do something. I spotted a Wal-Mart from the highway and pulled off at the exit determined to buy some insulated boots. Afraid of turning off the engine, I left the car running and hurried inside. I found some boots in my size. They looked warm and I envisioned the problem solved with warm and toasty feet all the rest of the way home. I slipped the boots on before leaving the store, carrying my old shoes in the boot sack and stowed them in the back of the car. But once back on the road it took only twenty minutes to realize the boots weren't as insulated as the claimed. It felt like needles were stabbing my toes as the cold became so intense, that I had to pull off at the next exit to warm up. That became my pattern. Every fifteen minutes on the road, I would have to pull off to warm up before getting back on the road. The McDonald's stops were the best. They had a hand dryer in their bathrooms that I could point down toward my feet. The warmth of the air blowing over them helped warm them back up quickly and I would get back on the road until the next exit. The exits were on average about every fifteen minutes apart. It extended the three-hour journey considerably, but I had no choice. By the time I reached the last exit to my hotel, it had been considerably further than fifteen minutes and my toes were in pain from the intense cold.

As I looked for a hotel, my mind was racing. What was I going to do about the Colt? I just wanted to get home. I decided I would leave the car running all night so as not to risk it not starting in the morning. I implemented my plan and filled up the gas tank. Then I went to the local Wal-Mart to get an extra key made. I couldn't feel my feet they were so numb and I struggled to walk the short distance into the store.

"Take your time," I told the attendant as he created the duplicate key. He looked at me kind of funny and then shrugged his shoulders. I doubt he heard that comment very often.

With the duplicate key in hand and a full tank, I pulled into the hotel parking lot and found a space close to the entrance in full view of the check-in window. I left the car running and checked in. "I'm going to leave my car running tonight," I told the hotel clerk as they handed me my key. I briefly explained the issue, hoping they would help keep watch of the car for me. But I was too tired to really care. I headed to my room with my bag in hand, ready for some heat and a bed. Within minutes I was fast asleep.

It was still dark out when the alarm went off. I got dressed quickly and hurried out my door. The Colt was still there and still running. Amazingly, it had used only a quarter of a tank during the night. I checked out of the hotel and jumped in the car, ready for another battle of endurance. But this time I knew every mile brought me further south into warmer temperatures and my family.

I had become an expert in the process by now as I got into the rhythm of tucking blankets, wiping the windshield and turning my head to exhale. It was almost as if there was a beat as I kept up the ongoing motion as my car ate up the miles. I made it home late that night, with the numbing cold of the north only a memory, welcoming the mild winter temperatures of Oklahoma.

I kissed Lavonne as I walked in the door and wrapped each of the kids in a big hug. "How was your trip, honey?" She asked. Boy, did I have a story to tell.

That trip will always be a reminder to me of God's protection. It was a hard trip, yet He was there every step of the way. The best news is that just five or six months into the start-up of our business, God made the way and I received contracts for orders from three different clients within a twenty-four-hour period! One of those was a direct result of the frigid no heater winter trip to North Dakota which I learned later had been a record low for the day I had been there!

Now we just had to come up with the capital to create the product and fill the orders, and the $200,000 to do it!

I wondered how God was going to do this one!

Chapter 12

I Needed a Bunch of Money How About $200,000?

I dressed up in my best suit and sat in the bank waiting to talk with a loan manager. The folder with the three contracts sat in my lap. The good news was I had real orders for my new system. The bad news was I needed money, and lots of it fast. In order to fill those first orders, I needed to purchase a van, expensive equipment and hardware to install in the vehicle. I had no money at all. Lavonne and I had been living by faith on an extremely lean budget for the last several months. In fact, our church food pantry provided our macaroni and cheese dinners during this season. We wouldn't have any income until we delivered on these contracts. I remembered seeing television ads for local area neighborhood banks which declared themselves as "small business friendly." Each night when the commercial ran it invited virtually anyone to come in for a friendly loan.

So here I sat, ready to be friendly.

The loan agent walked over and shook my hand. "How may I help you, Mr. Blanco?"

"You see, I have these contracts with buyers who want to buy these new systems from me," I began as I offered him the folder. "I just need a loan to buy the van, equipment, cameras, computers and everything that goes into the vehicle to fulfill the contract."

The manager took the folder from my hand and looked over the contracts as well as my loan application.

"How much equity do you have in your house?" he asked.

"Not much," I replied.

"How many cars do you have?"

"Just one," I responded. I didn't mention that it was a 1988 Colt with no heat.

"What does your wife do for a living?"

"She homeschools our four children," I answered, knowing that wasn't the answer he was looking for.

"So, she doesn't work? How much money do you need, Mr. Blanco?"

"I need $200,000."

That's where the conversation stopped. I learned from that "small business friendly" bank that I didn't have enough collateral to qualify for that big of a loan. In fact, the bank wanted several hundred thousand dollars of equity in my home or some other property in order to loan me that kind of money.

"But I have the signed contracts from my buyers that represent $400,000 in income," I countered pointing again at the contracts, but it didn't matter. Bank after bank turned me down in spite of the contracts guaranteeing the sale. Crossing the bank option off the list, I next went to friends who I thought might have those type of resources to see if they could offer a loan. One of our friends introduced us to one of their friends who they thought might be interested in just such an investment. We invited him over to meet with us. When I took him into the basement and showed him what I had worked on, he immediately caught the vision and saw the potential in the company. "Rudy, I'm in. I'll loan you the $200,000 you need to move forward," he said as we shook hands.

I was excited, but hesitant at the same time. Along with an investor came restrictions. He wanted a lot of interest for his investment and a lot of control in the company. But it seemed like an open door. In fact, it was our only option up to that point, so I took it before the Lord. "God, this is the only door that has opened. What do you want me to do? If you don't stop me, I'm going to go with this guy," I finished. I had the impression that it was okay to move ahead, so I called him and agreed to his terms.

"Great, go ahead and purchase the first vehicle, and I'll write you the check," he instructed. Now we were really in business.

I had my heart set on a red van. I called all around the Norman area, but couldn't find one so I stretched my search further and found one that seemed to fit our needs in the Dallas area. It seemed like the perfect "first" vehicle for us to introduce our new product for Pathway Services. I negotiated the price with the seller over the phone to what I felt was the best price I could get. "Great, I'll pick it up on Monday," I told him before we disconnected. I called the investor next to let him know that I had found a vehicle and would need to swing by his office, which was on the way to Dallas, so I could finalize the purchase.

"Can you have the check ready for me Monday morning?" I asked letting him know the amount.

"No problem, Rudy. I'll have it ready for you," he stated.

I have to admit I was pretty excited. This was the fulfillment of a dream. And after these first three contracts were filled, Lavonne and I would have some money available not only for the business, but so that I could start receiving some salary as well. It felt good. That is until Monday rolled around.

The phone rang as I was getting ready to leave for Dallas to pick up the new van. It was the investor. "Rudy, I'm sorry, I'm not going to be able to loan you the money after all. I talked with your former business partner over the weekend and he said he is going to sue you. I'm really sorry, but I don't think I'm going to do business with you."

I hung up the phone completely at a loss for words. I felt as if all the air had been punched out of me. Lavonne and I sat down at our kitchen table to talk it through. We were at that place where we had tried all the options we knew. Anything from here was going to have to be God. We prayed again. I sensed His calming voice speak to my heart, "I wanted you to try the world's system, Rudy. I wanted you to see how people normally do business without me involved. Now, sit back and watch how I get things done."

A blanket of peace seemed to descend on both Lavonne and I. We didn't know what God was going to do, but we knew He was going to do something. We sat and prayed over this situation as well. It would have been natural, I suppose, to be anxious about a potential threat of lawsuit, but I wasn't. I knew I was on the path God had opened for me and didn't spend a moment worrying about it. We just gave it over to God and decided to let Him deal with that issue as well. I had more important matters on my mind and the first was how to get that red van waiting for me in Dallas.

"Look, I don't have the cash after all," I told the salesman letting him know I still wanted to purchase the van. "Can we set it up on credit?"

The salesman put me on hold as he went to check with his sales manager and run my credit report. After several painstaking minutes he got back on the line. "We pulled your credit report and everything looks good. I'll draw up the paperwork and you can come pick it up."

Wow! That fast, and God had already done one miracle. We were going to be able to purchase the vehicle without having to pay exorbitant interest rates to an investor. That got the wheels in my head turning. If we could purchase the van on credit, what other credit might be available to us? We had only tried a large loan at a bank, but was there another way to go about this? Maybe there was a similar way to get our hands on the rest of the money we needed. During that time, it was unusual to get a credit card offer for a credit line with no interest for six months. But a few weeks earlier, I had received seven of them in the mail all about the same time. I went and opened those offers and began to study them. Suddenly, it dawned on me. A good portion of the money we needed was available here in these seven-credit card offers.

I worked to fill out the applications for all seven cards, and stuck then in the mail before Lavonne and I headed off for Dallas. Within a few weeks I received acceptance letters from all of them. I smiled at Lavonne as I held up the little pieces of plastic. I was not sure how or why seven different credit card companies approved me for that much credit, but I didn't care. I took it and we moved ahead recognizing it was a supernatural provision for that time.

The credit line we now had available from the seven credit cards was enough for us to begin buying the hardware and equipment we needed, but it wasn't enough. So, we reached out again to friends and family. Where before we couldn't seem to find anyone willing to assist us, that all had changed. Our pastor had sold his house and wouldn't be moving into his new home that was being built for several months. He offered to lend us $25,000, which we could use for three months. My wife's two brothers loaned us $5000 each. However, probably the biggest miracle was the loan that came from my father-in-law. Months earlier, when I was still working on writing the programs to launch our company and had no salary coming in, we hit a month in which we had trouble making our mortgage payment.

My father-in-law is a very frugal man, but I didn't know where else to turn at the time, so I called him with the request to loan us $500 for our mortgage that month. Although he didn't immediately agree, he eventually said yes, and gave us the loan. But about once a month since then I knew to expect a call from him. "Hey Rudy, where is my five hundred bucks?" he would ask. I hated being in debt, especially to family and looked forward to the day that the company could begin to pay me. But until then, we were grateful for the needed help.

In addition to the new credit cards we had just received and commitments from family and friends, we still lacked about $25,000 to continue to move forward to fulfill these first three contracts. As we sat at dinner one night I approached the subject with Lavonne about going to her father. "I'm not going to call him," she stated with a laugh. "You can call him if you want."

I asked Lavonne, "Why don't you call your mom and ask her if she knows what kind of money your dad has that we can ask him to loan us?" The worst he could do was say "no." She agreed and made the call.

Her mom told her she thought all he had in savings was around $25,000. "But don't tell him that I told you," she finished.

That was all I needed to know. I decided to go ahead and see if he would be willing to give us another loan. I knew it would be a miracle if he agreed.

"Hey, Wally," I began, but he immediately interrupted

"Are you going to pay me my $500?" he inquired.

"I wish," I responded. "But, you know Lavonne and I finally started our business and things are going well. In fact, we have several contracts already, but in order to fill them, we need some financial help to purchase the necessary equipment. Do you think you could loan us the money?" I held my breath as I waited for his response. I remembered how long it took him the last time I asked for money, and that was a small amount. A small amount I hadn't yet repaid.

"How much do you need?" he asked.

"Twenty-five thousand would be great," I responded surprised we were still in discussion.

He paused for just a second before saying, "Okay, I'll lend it to you."

I hung up the phone stunned. Had that just happened that fast? After he had pestered us to pay back the $500 on a monthly basis, now he was going to lend us all his savings. I was in awe as I was reminded of the words the Lord spoke to my heart, "Now, sit back and watch how I get things done." I was watching in amazement.

I finally had the resources to buy what I needed to outfit the first van, one piece at a time. But the even more amazing part of the miracle was it had been funded with no business partners, no bank loans and no one telling me how to run the business and the credit cards were all zero percent financing. Even with the money that we borrowed from friends and family they insisted that when we pay it back that we didn't have to pay interest. "Just pay me when you can," was the response from all of them. It was amazing.

One of the most unusual incidents at that time was one morning when I was leaving the house, I went to the front door and noticed a small brown grocery bag leaning against the wall by the door. When I opened it, inside was $500 in cash. This was just another confirmation that God was in control.

Essentially all the money ended up free to borrow. We filled all three contracts, received the payment and paid back all the debt within seven months…including my father-in-law's first loan of $500. The funny thing? He never once asked me when I would pay the $25,000 back, he only asked about the $500 loan.

Now that was God.

But that was just the beginning.

Chapter 13

NOT JUST ANY COMPANY

I didn't want to have a company, just to have a company. From the beginning, Lavonne and I had made a commitment to use the finances that God blessed us with to be a blessing to others. Now, as our company began to take off, this was especially true.

I recognized from the beginning that we were successful because God was driving things. This was His company; Lavonne and I were simply stewards. We watched as we turned the reigns over to Him, how He proved Himself time and again. We saw this happen in the first data collection vehicle we built.

Up to that time, my experience was that the customer would first order the product. Then it was up to me to order the materials and build it. The customer would then be invoiced upon delivery. Hopefully, we would be paid thirty days from delivery. It was expensive to build out those vans and so while each contract was welcomed, it also meant a huge outlay of funds initially. That is until we received the contract on our first data collection vehicle.

"How do you want to be paid," my client asked as we were completing the contract. I paused. I was about to tell him the usual process in which we would invoice him at the completion of the product, but what came out of my mouth was something quite different, "Can we do a percent complete arrangement?" I asked.

"I don't see why not," he responded. "Let me put it into the system and see if it goes through. I'll call you back," he said as we disconnected.

He called me back a few minutes later. "Yeah, Rudy it went through. No problem."

God just provided another miracle. That was a huge breakthrough for us. It meant we could invoice for the project as we completed portions of it. So, for example, when we had thirty percent completed, we sent him an invoice for that amount. That was huge. So, for this first vehicle, I was able to get installment payments as the project progressed, rather than needing to front all the money myself to fund the project. It was just another piece of the puzzle that God was putting together for us. This happened only once just at the beginning and just when we needed it the most.

The company began to grow as the orders grew, and I could no longer handle the process alone. God brought different team members from different places. One of the first to assist me was the dad of one of the girls on Mariana's soccer team.

If your child participates on some athletic team you know the drill. As parents, we faithfully show up to watch the games and sit together and talk. A new community develops as we meet these families and get to know them. It was through one of these discussions that I met Gary. He was a welder, and I needed a welder.

"Hey, do you think you would be able to help me if I had something I needed welded onto a vehicle?" I asked him one evening as we chatted at a game.

"Yeah, sure," he responded without giving it much thought.

In order to customize the vans with the data processing equipment for our orders, I had to install equipment into the vans. Each piece of equipment needed some type of brace or stand to hold it in place which had to be created. So, I would draw a rough sketch of what I needed and then drive it over to the welder's house. I held the sketch out to him to look over. "Can you make this?" I asked.

"Yeah, sure," he responded each time. I soon learned he was an amazing welder and nothing was too much of a challenge for him. As we began to put together the vehicles, he helped me attach a bar to the front bumper where we could connect sensors and lasers to scan the pavement as the vehicle drove the roads. We also ran wires from the front bumper, underneath the vehicle and back up into a hole we drilled in the van floor. We then attached the computer equipment and cameras to the wiring which we mounted in place with a rack he welded for me.

It was 1997 when we delivered our first vehicle. In addition to the data processing vehicles, I was also selling and delivering software orders. The orders for both were increasing quickly and I needed help.

We hired Michelle Newberg as our first full-time employee. She did a variety of tasks including acting as my secretary, receptionist, and purchasing manager, as well as buying the needed materials and equipment for the vans. A few months later, I hired our second full-time employee, Troy Mathews, who assisted with the building of the collection data vehicles. I was glad for the growth. Each team member added a new layer to the company as orders increased. I suppose we could have grown more quickly, but I chose to build step-by-step to ensure a high standard of quality and efficiency. God continued to bless it.

"What do you want me to do with this company?" I asked God not long after. The company was His. It was growing by leaps and bounds. I wanted to know His plan.

I was in the process of reading the Bible through for the second time when God pointed me to the story of Jacob's life in the book of Genesis. "Look what he did and what I did," I felt the Lord prompt.

Over the next few days I read the story of two twin brothers, Jacob and Esau in Genesis chapters 25-49. It was a story of greed, deception, forgiveness, blessing and promotion.

In the story the younger twin, Jacob, was favored by his mother, Rebekah; while his father, Isaac, favored his older twin, Esau. Even though Esau was just a few minutes older than his brother, he was still the oldest and according to Jewish tradition, he would be the one to receive the coveted blessing of his father as the first-born. Once the twins reached manhood, and as their father grew older, Rebekah recognized that the day of blessing had arrived. She was determined that her favorite, Jacob, would receive the blessing and concocted an elaborate scheme to steal the blessing from Esau. A prophecy had been spoken before the boy's birth that the older would serve the younger. Rebekah had never forgotten that and launched her scheme. Her plan worked, and Jacob deceptively received the blessing of the first-born, but he also received his brother's hatred.

Esau's anger burned and he sought to kill his brother. Once again Rebekah intervened to manipulate the situation and yet even in her deception and intervention, God had a bigger plan. He always does.

In Genesis 27:42-46 it says, *"When Rebekah was told what her older son Esau had said, she sent for her younger son Jacob and said to him, 'Your brother Esau is planning to avenge himself by killing you. Now then, my son, do what I say: Flee at once to my brother Laban in Harran. Stay with him for a while until your brother's fury subsides. When your brother is no longer angry with you and forgets what you did to him, I'll send word for you to come back from there. Why should I lose both of you in one day?'*

Then Rebekah said to Isaac, 'I'm disgusted with living because of these Hittite women. If Jacob takes a wife from among the women of this land, from Hittite women like these, my life will not be worth living.'"

Rebekah's plan was simply to get Jacob out of town until Esau cooled off. But what happened next set the course for Jacob's life as God's plan superseded Rebekah's and Jacob was forever changed. Isaac called Jacob to come to him and gave him instruction to travel to his uncle's home to find a wife. Even in this God was guiding him and blessing him for Isaac's blessing rested upon him.

As he journeyed to his uncle's home, one night along the way he had a vision. Afterwards the Lord spoke to him, *"Your descendants will be like the dust of the earth, and you will spread out to the west and to the east, to the north and to the south. All peoples on earth will be blessed through you and your offspring. I am with you and will watch over you wherever you go, and I will bring you back to this land. I will not leave you until I have done what I have promised you."5*

Jacob recognized the significance of what had happened and made a promise to God the next morning, *"If God will be with me and will watch over me on this journey I am taking and will give me food to eat and clothes to wear so that I return safely to my father's household, then the Lord[f] will be my God and this stone that I have set up as a pillar will be God's house, and of all that you give me I will give you a tenth."6*

I couldn't take my mind off of the vow Jacob had made to God, "If you will be with me and watch over me, (which to me meant he would give me protection), and will give me food and clothing—(provision) of all that you give me I will give you a tenth."8 That really stood out to me. Lavonne and I had always determined to give a portion of our income back to God to help others. We had seen how God had blessed those efforts. Yet, the company was in such an infancy stage that I also struggled with the decision. It was hard to give when there didn't seem to be any extra to give. I needed every dollar to purchase more sensors and cameras, not to mention the need for additional employees. It just seemed like a huge request God was making when I sensed him tell me, "I want the *first* ten percent right off the top, just like Jacob promised." I discovered He was still teaching and testing me about walking by faith.

So Jacob found his uncle's home quite miraculously and was welcomed in. He quickly fell in love with his uncle Laban's youngest daughter and worked for her hand in marriage.

Jacob, who deceived his father, spent the next twenty years working for his Uncle Laban, who deceived him over and over again. But in spite of the lies, cheating, and changed wages that Laban did to take advantage of Jacob, instead God blessed Jacob just as he promised in the vision. We can see that in this verse where it says, *"In this way the man grew exceedingly prosperous and came to own large flocks, and female and male servants, and camels and donkeys."*[7]

In Deuteronomy 26:1-19 the people were instructed to take part of the first produce of their harvest, put it into a basket and offer it to the priests. If they did that, the Lord promised His blessing would follow.

> *"When you have entered the land the Lord your God is giving you as an inheritance and have taken possession of it and settled in it, take some of the first fruits of all that you produce from the soil of the land the Lord your God is giving you and put them in a basket. Then go to the place the Lord your God will choose as a dwelling for his Name and say to the priest in office at the time, "I declare today to the Lord your God that I have come to the land the Lord swore to our ancestors to give us." The priest shall take the basket from your hands and set it down in front of the altar of the Lord your God.*[9]*"*

I thought back to when Lavonne and I had pledged to give fifty percent of our income on those extra projects that had come in while I worked in

Spokane. God had blessed us as wc had given him fifty percent of the extra income. But now he was asking for something different. He wanted the first ten percent off the top. I began to negotiate with Him. You know, I don't think God gets angry with us when we have discussions like that with Him. He was teaching me and I found He is a patient teacher.

"Wouldn't fifty percent of the profit be better?" I questioned.

"No, I want ten percent of the gross income of every dollar that comes into the company not just from the profit," I sensed Him respond. It was about honoring Him and putting Him first.

After a while, I finally understood what He was asking me. When I gave God out of my profit, I was really giving Him my leftovers after everything else was paid first. God didn't want leftovers. He wanted to be first. As any business owner knows, when it comes to taxes, we want to show as much expenditure as possible to reduce what appears as overall profit on our tax returns. He wants first place in our finances and our hearts. It was a big decision for me to make that change. And as you can imagine, it didn't come without a challenge.

During this struggle I had with God about what I felt He was asking of me, I was hit with a lawsuit from my former business partner. I realized I needed protection.

Lavonne and I immediately took the issue to the Lord. I had never been named in a lawsuit before and had no idea what to do. All I knew was that I needed God's protection.

I thought back to the story of Jacob I had just read. Jacob worked for his Uncle Laban for twenty-five years. During those years Laban changed the wages several times, lied to him, deceived him and cheated him by telling Jacob he could marry his youngest daughter, whom Jacob had fallen in love with. However, on the wedding night, Laban switched out the older daughter for the younger. Jacob the deceiver had been deceived. He had already worked seven years for the beautiful Rachel, but ended up with the not-so-beautiful, older sister Leah. Laban then made a deal with him. Work for me seven more years, and I will give you Rachel after one week. Jacob agreed. However, Laban continued to lie and cheat Jacob over the years. But no matter what he did, God blessed Jacob. As the devious practices of his uncle continued, Jacob knew he and his family had to leave. Laban wasn't happy at all. He knew he had been blessed because Jacob had worked for him.

I felt my story had many parallels to the story of Jacob. I knew I had done the right thing. So, Lavonne and I turned the matter over to the Lord, trusting that He would take care of us and protect us as he had taken care of Jacob.

We decided to look for a lawyer to represent us. We met with one and showed him our contract and correspondence during the time I worked for the previous company. He and some other lawyers looked the contract over and then he got back with me. "Yes, I can take the case, but it will require a $10,000 retainer to start."

I was shocked. Ten grand just to start? As I walked out the door of his office, I heard God speak clearly to my heart, "Rudy, you have been struggling with me about giving me the first fruits offering. So, you have a choice. Do you want to give your money to them to protect you, or do you want to trust Me to protect you? If you put your trust in Me, I will handle this. I have proven Myself to you already over and over. I'm your advocate. I will be your lawyer," he finished.

It was an easy decision at that point. I chose God. The funny thing is, after I made that decision, it was never a struggle again.

The lawsuit was settled out of court. God had taken care of it as He had promised. As our business partner, I watched as He protected us over and over from things we didn't even know were a problem.

For example, sometimes I would pray to get a specific contract for the company, and yet we wouldn't get it. At first that confused me. "Why

God?" I asked when the contract went to another company. Sometime later I found out that the contract had turned into a nightmare for the company that had received it. God had actually been protecting us from a problem that we couldn't see. As we have invited Him into every aspect of the business, we have seen His blessings multiply as He has brought the right people at the right time to add to our company, or the right opportunities, growing the business in ways I could have never imagined. In twenty years, the company has grown far bigger than I could have ever dreamed.

As God was growing our business, we discovered our family was about to grow in new ways as well.

Chapter 14

ADOPTION IS THE OPTION

As our four kids grew, we included them in various aspects of the company. When they were middle school age and high school, they would assist us with copying the video tapes which constantly came in from the vans. It wasn't a hard job, but required two-hour cycle monitoring. The kids got the idea to turn this job into a shared project and would often invite several of their friends to come to a sleep over at the office. They would eat pizza, play games and make copies of the video tapes. My oldest daughter, Mariana was in charge of setting the alarm clock every two hours through the night to remove the copied video tapes and insert new ones. As you can imagine, the newness of that job lost its luster fairly quickly and she was glad when we hired more staff and turned that task over to someone else.

Our kids were all getting older and I could see that "empty nest" phase fast approaching. Our oldest Mariana was now twenty-two, Diana was twenty, Daniel was sixteen and Mark was fourteen. I was looking forward to the day that college would be all paid for and for the opportunity to kick back and relax a little bit more.

Then one morning in 2002, Lavonne rolled over in bed. "Rudy, are you awake?" she asked me.

"I am now," I replied, although I already was, but not yet ready to get out of bed.

"We're still young," she began.

"Uh oh," I thought. "This doesn't sound good. Where is this going?"

"I think we should consider adopting," she stated.

I stared at her trying to focus my eyes and my mind around what she had just said. But no words came. I was speechless.

I hoped this new idea Lavonne had would go away, but it didn't. In fact, she brought it up once a day for the next *seven* days. "Surely, she will come to her senses," I thought and tried to ignore her. But this wasn't some fad idea within Lavonne. She had an overwhelming sense within her that our family wasn't complete.

The more she talked about her idea, it reminded me of a few years before when we had met and become friends with a family that had twelve kids. Six natural born and six adopted. We were in a Bible study together and so we interacted with them almost every week. That's a lot of kids, and yet what I remember most vividly about this family was the love and harmony in which they worked together. It was quite remarkable.

I didn't know many families who had adopted when I grew up in Costa Rica. It just wasn't common there. But the more Lavonne talked about it, the more the idea simmered in my heart until one day I woke up and thought, "Why not?" I had seen it work with the family we had known. We had always had a desire to bless others. Why not make it personal and be a blessing to a child that had no parents?

As I meditated on the thought further, I sought the Lord for confirmation if this idea was from Him. Adopting a child is a huge commitment and a decision that I didn't take lightly. "Lord, if this is of you, please confirm it to us and give me peace."

We started by making some initial queries into the process on what it would take to adopt. We called some adoption agencies to learn more about the process, the cost, and where there might be children available. We discovered there are numerous agencies out there and they were happy to provide us with the information. We learned there was an excellent firm right in our city called Dillon International. We discovered people we knew who had used and highly recommended the agency, so we contacted them.

"There are five primary countries from which you might adopt: India, Haiti, China, Guatemala and the Ukraine," the worker informed us as we inquired about their services. When they said Ukraine, something sparked within me. It just seemed right. I know that might not make much sense, since Lavonne and I both spoke Spanish, but it was what I sensed in my spirit. Yet, I still wanted confirmation if this was the direction in which the Lord wanted us to proceed.

About that time, I was on a business trip flying home from San Diego. Air travel is a great time for reflection and prayer. As I settled into my seat, I remember praying and asking God about the adoption option. Once we took off, I opened a copy of *The Wall Street Journal* that I had purchased before boarding at one of the airport stores As I scanned the list of article titles on the editorial page, one jumped out at me, "Two Ukrainians…"

Chills ran down my spine. That was a confirmation for me. Immediately I felt confident we were supposed to adopt from the Ukraine, But, now I wondered, would we be adopting one or maybe two?

Lavonne and I completed the necessary paperwork to begin the adoption process. It was extensive. Afterwards, we were required to do a "home study" in which a case worker did research into our home and family. It took approximately four months as they researched information on our family background and references, education, employment, daily life rou-tines, parenting practices, relationships within our family and our readiness to adopt. It took almost a year for us to get everything completed and submitted. It was during this entire process that we had another major decision to make. It looked like we needed to move the company.

Chapter 15

UNBELIEVABLE EXPANSION

At the end of the first nine months, after we birthed and launched the business from our basement, the company took off. We couldn't keep the company in our basement any longer. That's when a friend told us of a property for sale in Noble, Oklahoma which was approximately ten miles from Norman. It was a 5000 square foot former church building. Initially it had fit our needs perfectly as we slowly started to add employees and build out the vehicles that had been ordered. Over the next couple of years as the business grew, we added on to the building so that it was now 11,000 square feet, but even with that addition, we were quickly outgrowing it as we added new employees and the orders increased. I had looked all over Norman for a larger, suitable facility, but there didn't seem to be anything available. We had also started to search in the neighboring city of Edmond. It seemed like the logical choice, but in my heart, it didn't feel right. One day as I was pacing back and forth Lavonne stopped me.

"Rudy, what's wrong? You're going to wear out the carpet."

"Honey, I keep thinking we are supposed to move the company to Tulsa."

"Tulsa? Rudy, that would involve moving the kids to a different school and uprooting everyone and starting over again. Are you sure?"

The more I prayed about it the more I sensed that we were to be in Tulsa. But I also knew it wouldn't be an easy move.

"Why don't we just make a trip there," I suggested to Lavonne. "If they don't have any facilities that meet our needs, then we'll know it's not the place for us."

So we made the two hour drive to Tulsa to check it out. It was a productive trip. Although, there wasn't a building in Tulsa proper, in a smaller suburb next to Tulsa we found a facility that was perfect for our needs. It was approximately 18,000 square feet and would give us some space to grow. Located in an industrial park, it was ideally suited for our needs to take the company to the next level. In fact, if I had custom designed my own building that would have been it. In addition, we already knew of a private school in the area where we could transfer the kids to complete their educations. It was as if God had already taken care of every detail for us to make this move.

We didn't know how long the adoption process would take as our paperwork was getting reviewed and so we went ahead and started packing to relocate to Tulsa. Several of our employees made the move with us. We were grateful that they wanted to stay with us. As I had written in my company vision for Sonrise Foods years before, I recognized that the employees of a company are its most valuable assets. That's certainly how Lavonne and I felt about our staff, and we were excited that we would not be starting from scratch to replace them.

A few years before, God had also opened the door for us to open an office in Costa Rica that processed our data. Our vans would go to a state and drive every single road in the state. The sensors and equipment loaded on the vans would then take that information and create an automated individualized report for each state. But all of that data had to be processed, analyzed and checked for quality. It was an in-depth job, and required lots of man hours to process that information into reports for the client. We had the idea that if we could open a company in Costa Rica to provide these services to Pathway Services, it could be a blessing to my family and the people there. So that's exactly what we did. My sister, Vyria, managed the company for us, and I traveled there to help initially train the workers to do the important labor-intensive data analysis for us. It was wonderful working with my sister and in my home country, which was another dream fulfilled. God had been so good to us.

In keeping with our original vision to bless others, we shared that concept with our employees in our Costa Rica branch. It resonated deeply with them and they took ownership of it. For example, they launched plans to have an annual Christmas party in which each worker in the company would choose or "adopt" a very poor family in the community. They would then invite them and their family to the Christmas party which lasted all day. Using the "first fruits" offering of the company, we would provide food, gifts for the entire family, games, and a festive atmosphere. When the party was over, they left with gifts and food to take with them. It became one of the highlights each year for our Costa Rican office. Now they deliver food monthly, they have provided houses for the poor, contribute to orphanages, and handicap homes, among other things. The Christmas party became a launching pad to see the greatest needs in the community and act on them.

It had been about a year since we relocated the company and our family to Tulsa when it came time for Mariana to graduate. She had been attending the University of Southern California in Los Angeles and would graduate with her degree in Computer Science and Film Studies. I thought back to those early years as she worked so faithfully to help us copy the data video tapes for the company. Her gift for screenwriting and video had shown up early as she would sometimes assist us with our annual Christmas letter to friends and family. The years that Mariana took on the project as the writer for the family were great. She would produce a light-hearted, humorous script. I remember one Christmas newsletter in particular from the Blanco family. Mariana had taken on the project that year which read like a movie script.

WHERE ARE THEY NOW?

FADE TO: INT. Office at Pathway Services. Rudy sits in a nice large office chair in the middle of a nice large office decorated with many piles of paper, wires and computers.

NARRATOR: "How has your last year been?"

RUDY (calmly): "Guud."

DIANA walks in. DANNY walks in. LAVONNE walks in. MARK walks in. SEVERAL employees walk in. They chorus together:

"Where does this go?" "Where do you want the 3424y32dke28 monitor?" "Mr. Nebraska's on the phone for you." "The bathrooms clean." "How do you do this?"

NARRATOR: "And soccer?"

RUDY (calmly): "Guud."

I smiled as I considered the fun and humor she brought to our family through her gift.

Now, as she prepared to accept her degree and launch into a new season of life, it was with that bittersweet feeling with which almost all parents struggle. We were so proud of her and all she had accomplished, and yet to pursue her career, she would remain in California. Darn!

We packed up the family and we all flew down to be part of the graduation that weekend. It was while we were there that I received a phone call from my sister, Vyria. "Rodolfo, you better find a place to sit down. Our brother Carlos was in a car accident. He is dead."

I hung up the phone stunned. It was such devastating news. My mind immediately raced to all the memories stored up over the years such as when Carlos taught me how to drive a caterpillar bulldozer in the Costa Rican jungles when I was fourteen years old. How in his effort to welcome Lavonne into our family he would take the extra effort on a regular basis to drive by the house, toot his horn and motion her to the gate where he would hand her a mango or some piece of fruit. One of the most vivid memories was the time when I finally did join my brothers at the swimming pool. The only problem was not only did I not know how to swim, I didn't even know that you needed to know how to swim! I changed into the swim trunks and ran out to the deep end of the pool where I jumped into the deepest part. I immediately began to struggle and take in water. Carlos was right there as he jumped in and pulled me out to rescue me.

"Are you crazy? You don't even know how to swim and you went into the deep end," he reprimanded me with fatherly concern. I could see the fear in his eyes and recognized he had saved my life.

Carlos was more than just an older sibling. When Dad had passed away, he had matured overnight as he stepped up to take responsibility for the family and help Mom. During those years he had made sure we all stayed in school and helped many of us get through college. Although only in his late teens himself at that time, he had been more like a father figure to me than an older brother and I wept knowing that he was now gone.

We immediately made plans to fly back to Costa Rica to be with the family. We arrived in time for the funeral. This was a significant reminder of how quickly life can change and how we have to be prepared. I believe the main preparation is the spiritual preparation and the condition of our hearts. We are never guaranteed another day and life can end unexpectedly. It's a sobering thought and one that begs the question, "If you died today, where would *you* spend eternity?"

"What about Carlos, God?" I remember asking after I learned of his death. He was the only one of my siblings that I wasn't certain if he had accepted God into his life. Yet in that moment God gave me assurance in my heart that he had made that decision as he took me back to the last time I had been to Costa Rica. Carlos and I had spent the day together. Part of that was driving in his car doing errands. I remember distinctly how surprised I was that he had Christian music playing from the radio station—and it wasn't for my benefit. No, something had changed in his life the last year, and I sensed His peace fill me that one day again I would see my brother Carlos in heaven. I started this journey with the Lord when I answered an invitation from the pastor at the "church on the hill" that Easter Sunday when we lived in Spokane, WA so many years ago. Now, to me death has no sting. Like the scripture says in I Corinthians 15:55-57, *"Where, O death, is your victory? Where, O death, is your sting?" The sting of death is sin, and the power of sin is the law. But thanks be to God! He gives us the victory through our Lord Jesus Christ."*

I am so looking forward to that day, because I will just continue this exciting journey I am living with the Lord.

So, if someone asked you that question today, "Where will you spend eternity after you die?" If you don't know the answer to that question, but want to be sure you will be in heaven with Him, the Bible tells us very clearly in Romans 10:9, *"If you declare with your mouth, 'Jesus is Lord,' and believe in your heart that God raised him from the dead, you will be saved."*

So, all we have to do is to believe in our hearts that God raised Jesus Christ from the dead after He was crucified for all our sins, and to confess with our mouth, "that Jesus is Lord." God gave His Son for us because of His love for us.

The moment we do this, we are saved and no one can take that away from us.

There was a time in my life when I couldn't with certainty, answer that question, and it made me afraid. But I learned during this long road from Costa Rica to Oklahoma that God is good and He loves me. I don't have to live with fear or doubt now or beyond.

After our return from Costa Rica, our lives shifted into the adoption process. When we had submitted our paperwork to be considered by the adoption agencies, we were told it would take about three months to hear back. It had already been eight months and it had taken a year prior to that just to submit the paperwork in the first place. So almost two years had passed since Lavonne first felt we were to adopt.

"Lord, I'm not getting any younger," I told him one day as I continued to ponder and pray about the possibility of adopting. "Please either do it now or we're going to need to think about scrapping this idea."

It was now 2004 and just about the time we thought we had missed God's will, we received a phone call from our contact at Dillon International. "Hey Rudy, they've processed your application at the Ukraine agency and have an appointment for you and Lavonne. Can you be ready to go in a week?"

In order to move the process forward, it required that Lavonne and I fly to Ukraine, go to the adoption agency on that side, and complete the final paperwork for consideration. Then we would just have to wait. The really hard part was that we were told that there was no guarantee that we would leave with a child. We might make the trip for nothing.

Yet still, Lavonne and I felt that this was God's plan for us and so we bought our tickets, and I worked to get things in order so that I could be out of the office for a couple of weeks. That in itself was no small thing.

We brought a friend from Tulsa with us who could serve as a translator. It turns out when we arrived, that they appointed a translator of their own to help us. We completed the required paperwork with the request for two children. That was truly a step of faith for us. It turns out, if we had requested just one, we would have been sent home empty-handed.

Chapter 16

WHERE DOES THE JOURNEY LEAD?

We sat down at the table with the orphanage worker and watched as she brought out a book full of photographs of the children who were available. Our hopes soared. This looked promising. We had been advised by several people that we should adopt a child five or under due to abandonment issues that are usually present in older children. We didn't want a newborn and so on our application we had requested one or two children between the ages of three and five. But as we flipped through the pages of the book before us to study the images of the children, we discovered that there was not a single child available in that age range. It was hard to believe.

"Well, you did say that you would be willing to take two. Correct?" The worker verified as she got up from the table. She walked over to the shelf, studied the notebooks before her and then pulled one off. She brought it back over to the table and laid it before us. "The only thing we have left is our book of siblings. Let's see what we can find there," she stated as she opened to the first page.

At first it appeared that once again, no children were available, but then as we continued to look she stopped us. "Ah, yes, these two are available," she stated as she pulled the page out of the binder and set it on the table in front of us. About that time, Lavonne turned to me in an almost panicked state, "Rudy, how on earth are we going to choose?" she asked as she looked intently at the pictures flipping the pages back and forth.

I didn't know. It was overwhelming.

"I can't do this, Rudy. I can't," Lavonne said. "You're going to have to choose."

"Lord, please help us. Show us who is Your choice for our family," I prayed as the worker continued to turn the pages. I remember when the book fell open to a page of a brother and sister. It was almost as if their two faces just popped out at me in brilliant color against a field of grey. It was so vivid.

"I think these are our two kids right here," I told myself as I looked at them. Something inside me was telling me that it was those two.

As the worker finished showing us all the pages in the book of siblings, we ended up with five pairs of siblings.

"Let me see which ones are still available," the worker stated as she flipped through their paperwork. She excused herself and went to make phone calls to their respective orphanages in order to verify their status and determine if they were still available or not.

Lavonne and I waited at the table alternating between crossing our legs and tapping the table...anything to make the time go faster. We looked at each other and I knew we were asking ourselves the same question, "How do we choose which children to help and ignore the rest?" All these kids needed and deserved parents.

It seemed to take forever, but finally she hung up the phone and walked back over to where we were seated.

"Okay, these are not available," she said as she turned over the photographs of one set of siblings. "And neither are these," she said as she turned another page over, removing them from selection. Page after page the worker went through turning them over onto the "not available" pile. Every set of siblings was now no longer available except one—the brother and sister whose picture had seemed to stand out so vividly a few moments before.

"These two are available," she said as she laid their pictures in front of us. "Do you still want them?" she asked.

"Yes! Yes!" Lavonne and I declared in unison. We knew instantly that these were our kids.

"Okay, we'll need you to get ready for an overnight train to Kharkiv," the woman said. "That's where their orphanage is located."

Kharkiv was a twelve-hour train ride from Kiev the capital of Ukraine, on a "hard sleeper" overnight train. Forget any vision of a romantic train ride through lush landscape. That was not this experience. In fact, we were explicitly instructed to lock our doors and not to open them under any condition!

As it turns out, of the five siblings that appeared available in the paperwork, the *only* ones that were actually available were the brother and sister that had seemed to pop out at me. Even more interesting was that their files for adoption had only been approved the day before. We learned there is a waiting process once a child enters the orphanage to make sure that there isn't a father, mother or grandparents who show up later to claim them. That waiting period had just ended for these two the day before. Had we come even one day earlier, we would not have been able to adopt them.

We also learned that there had been another component in this adoption selection, one that still amazes us to this day. After we signed the

135

papers choosing Lynna and Austin to be adopted, we left for the day. Our friend who had accompanied us and was also acting as a translator filled us in on a conversation the orphanage workers shared with her while we were there. In the last couple of weeks, they had become very concerned about Lynna and her brother Austin. They mentioned that during that time something had changed within Lynna and daily she began to ask, "When are my parents coming?"

The thing was, that although we were far into the adoption process as far as paperwork, no child(ren) had been chosen for us yet. She didn't know we existed at that point, and we certainly didn't know anything about any specific children at that point. She couldn't have known that we were coming for her, because that connection hadn't yet been made and yet she continued to ask the workers daily, "When are my parents coming?"

This continued daily for the next two weeks. Finally, concerned for her emotional well-being, one of the orphanage workers asked her what made her think her parents were on the way.

Lynna then explained how she had seen a picture of the Madonna with the Christ child from one of the other care givers whom she loved very much. Something from that Russian orthodox photo of Mary holding baby Jesus resonated deeply within her heart. Even as a child she understood that Jesus was God. Fed up with the orphanage and not having parents she got down on her knees and prayed, "I don't want to be in the orphanage, would you please send me parents?" From the depths of her heart she prayed a prayer of faith to a God she didn't know, but who knew her and loved her. And in that moment, something began to happen as the application process drawing us to her accelerated.

Two weeks later, we walked into that orphanage to pick her up along with her brother. Oh, the powerful faith of a child! In the end, we didn't choose Lynna and Austin, God chose them for us because of her prayer.

Austin (5) and Lynna (7) adjusted well into our family. I can only chuckle as I look back over that season in which they not only learned

WHERE DOES THE JOURNEY LEAD?

English quickly, but also Spanish. Within thirty days after their arrival to our home in the States, we packed them up and took them to Costa Rica to meet my family. We stayed there about a month. I think now of all they processed during those first thirty days between English, the American culture, and Spanish and the Costa Rican culture. Somewhere their little pliable minds were able to make sense of it all. I remember Austin coming out with some sentences that had a mixture of Russian, English and Spanish words all rolled into it in those first few weeks. But very quickly they both were able to sort it through, and were communicating with us all.

Sometime after that, I began to consider the age gap between our youngest, Mark who was now sixteen, and Lynna who was seven.

"Lavonne, I bet we could squeeze one child more into that space and fill the gap. What do you think?"

We looked at each other for a moment. I'm sure her mind was whirling as was mine with the thought of all the logistics and paperwork that would have to be undertaken again to make that happen and almost as quickly as I had said it, we passed on that idea. Adopting Austin and Lynna had been a two year, rather daunting process and while we were so glad to have them as part of our family, the thought of doing it all over again held little appeal. "God if you want us to have another child," I remember praying, "Then he or she will have to come knock on our door."

And that's exactly what happened…

Chapter 17

A KNOCK AT OUR DOOR

The phone rang. I'm sure I had a most unusual expression on my face as I listened to the request of the caller. As I hung up the phone, I turned to Lavonne. "Who was it," she asked.

"It was this ministry that works with kids that are about to age out of the orphanages," I replied.

We had learned about "aging out" as we adopted Lynna and Austin. For kids that are never adopted, once they reach a certain age, and for some orphanages that is as young as fifteen, then they are released from the orphanage. With little to no education their hope of finding a job, shelter, food and safety is minimal. These are kids who life has overlooked. Many end up selling themselves just to live. The average age expectancy for these kids after leaving the orphanage is just two years. The ministry who called us was now targeting their efforts to help these children. And they were targeting us!

"They are bringing a group of kids in from Russia for a ten-day trip in a couple of months and wanted to know if we would be a host family for one of the girls?" I explained to Lavonne from what I had learned on the call, but there were more questions than answers at that point.

The kids that this ministry worked with were not only aging out of the system, but they were also handicapped, which is why many of them had not been adopted. The ministry wanted to do everything in their power to give these kids a chance at something better. The kids were excited as they prepared for a once-in-a-life time trip to America. But in actuality, what they didn't know was that it was a last-ditch effort to save their lives as the ministry hoped that by connecting them with a host family that they were in reality connecting them with their forever family.

Lavonne and I were well aware of the responsibility we were undertaking if we said "yes" to the opportunity before us.

Knock. Knock. Knock.

Just a couple months later Katya knocked on our door along with one of the ministry workers. She was fourteen years old with short brown hair, a timid girl who we later discovered had a lot of spunk. She was constantly singing as she was with us during those ten days. But literally, this girl came to our house and knocked on the door.

Katya spent the next two weeks with us. We took her around the city and attended the activities the ministry had set up with the other families for a basketball game, a picnic and other events.

When the two weeks were over Katya had to return home.

From the time the phone call from the ministry first came until Katya left we had never talked about the elephant in the room. Lavonne and I both knew that you don't take a child like that in unless you are serious about adopting them. It really had never been a question for us, we opened our door and our arms. After she left, Lavonne immediately turned to me with a smile on her face, "Should I start the paperwork now?"

We decided to call her Katie and her adoption was so much quicker and easier than Lynna and Austin's. The paperwork time was cut to six months largely because Lavonne was traveling back and forth to Costa Rica at the time to be with Lynna and Austin. We had decided to let them live with my family in Costa Rica for the school year, so that they could learn Spanish. Lavonne split her time being with them in Costa Rica and being with us in the U.S. that year. Now with Katie's adoption paperwork, she would work fervently to get each set of papers completed and finished between her trips. As she submitted the next section, she would inform them that she was leaving for Costa Rica. What we discovered was that the trips seemed to expedite the process as the agencies on both sides worked to accommodate Lavonne's travel schedule. In just six months the paperwork had been completed and approved for Katie to join our family!

While we had hosted her in our home six months prior, our Russian friend, Luba, who had been our translator with Austin and Lynna's adoption, had come over to visit with Katie during her ten day stay. Katie appreciated having someone to converse with in her own language and beamed as our friend handed her two music CD's. They were by a Ukranian singer named Valentina, who was a Christian singer that lived in Washington state. They quickly became a treasured possession. We bought Katie a CD player with a strap, so that she could sling the machine over her shoulder and carry it with her. She played that CD over and over learning the songs by heart. She continued to listen to them during the six months after returning to Russia while we completed the paperwork. We were about to learn just how important that CD of songs had been in Katie's life.

"Mrs. Blanco, the paperwork is complete and you need to leave for Russia in one week to complete the adoption papers and pick up Katya," we were informed by the agency here in the States. Everything went into high gear now as we made preparations to make sure all our kids were taken care of, as well as the business in our absence. Ingrid, our niece stepped in to watch over Lynna and Austin in Costa Rica. She had been a godsend and had become like a second mother to them while they were spending the school year there to learn Spanish. Our youngest, Mark was now in college which meant our biological kids were now all grown and so it was relatively easy to make sure any needs they had were taken care of as we prepared to go. The business was another story, but by now we had a staff of workers that kept things running smoothly. We packed, and had tickets in hand ready to go in just seven days with the assurance that once again God was orchestrating our steps.

After flying to Moscow, we then took an overnight train to the city of Chuvashia. The orphanage workers drove Katie to the hotel where we were staying, and handed her over to us. But we weren't quite finished. Our next step was to go before a judge to make it official, and then we would have to work on her passport and documents. As it happened, the day we went before the judge and the adoption became official, was July 9, Katie's birthday. We did not know that or try to orchestrate it. It was all God's doing. For her fifteenth birthday that year, Katie received a mother, father, and siblings!

We knew there was a transition process ahead—the language barrier for one. The very first night she was with us, she immediately began to try to communicate with us something which we could tell was obviously important to her. That was when we realized the blessing of the CD she had been given by our friend. Although there had been no one in the orphanage to teach her about God, the songs of the CD and the Christian singer Valentina, had done it through the songs that she had soaked in for the last six months. They had changed her life. We now understood through lots of hand motions as she pointed to the CD and the phone number listed on the case that she wanted us to call Valentina so they could talk.

"Katie, I can't until we get to the States. It's too expensive from here," I tried to communicate between English and hand signals. This was long before mobile phones. So, an international call while possible, would have been expensive. "We will do it as soon as we get back," I tried to explain. She was satisfied enough, but barely.

As soon as we got to America, Katie continued to let us know how important that call was to her. Daily, she brought it to our attention. While we couldn't read the CD label which was all in Russian, I could tell that the phone number was within the states. The only problem was the last digit of the number was partially cut off, so it was almost impossible to tell what it should have been. I tried a multitude of combinations, but couldn't tell if any of them were the right number. I didn't get an answer or answering machine that gave me any indication which number might be correct.

One day as we were over in my office, Katie and Lavonne came in. Katie immediately came over to me. After giving me a hug, she held the CD out again and tapped at the phone number. "Papa, call!" she requested. She was persistent, I'll give her that. I smiled as I sat down at my desk and dialed the number—well at least one of the possible combinations it could have been—and handed the phone to Katie. The next thing I remember is hearing Katie's excited voice as she began to chatter in Russian. This time the call had connected her to Valentina herself. Katie's smile and excitement filled my heart with joy. God had given us a girl that He had already drawn to Himself and prepared her for us. We needed God's help as much as she needed our help.

Katie's entrance into our family, like Lynna and Austin, had been God ordained. Now several years later, it is hard to believe how perfectly they fit in, and completed our family.

As I look back over this journey of life and those adoptions, I see His hand ordering and directing our steps in His perfect time table. It has been an incredible journey, one that is not over for us. In reality, it is just beginning.

Each one of us is at a different point in our journey on this earth, but when we put it into the perspective of eternity, our journeys are just beginning.

I am convinced that God wants to "hang out" with you and me now and forever. That is the reason He created us. He keeps telling that to us in His Word and that is why I want you to read the second part of this book.

Beyond today, there eternity is waiting. With God, our future is an exciting journey.

So, don't go away—go beyond!

Go to Part II.

A Note from Lavonne

I marvel as I consider the impact that Rudy has made, and how his willingness to walk in obedience to God has not only affected our life and marriage together, but it has left a legacy for our children.

All the older kids are adults and each has an entrepreneurial spirit. I think watching and working with their father growing up they saw his "never give up" attitude and perseverance even when things got hard. They have heard the stories of those early years as we trusted God for finances when he continued to work with no paycheck coming in and yet as we determined to trust God, and stay with our commitment to give away half of the money that came in through "extra" jobs even when that really was our only income for a season.

They have watched with front row seats as God has developed and used the gift within Rudy to create and build a business that has been a blessing to many. I believe it cast vision in their lives to reach for the stars and to not be afraid to run for your dream using the talents that God gave them.

All of the kids have a strong sense of generosity as well. It warms my heart to watch them give at their level. Even the littlest will invite anyone and everyone to come eat with us or to share whatever they have. They have a perseverance within them and understand that it takes time to develop something well. Once they set their minds to do something, they stay after it.

As some of our kids have married, I have seen even their choice of a mate reflect these interests. Both of our daughters-in-law and son-in-law have a heart for missions work overseas to bless others that are less fortunate. Our daughter, Diana and her husband, Josh have adopted a child from Tanzania and the others may well follow in those footsteps.

Would that have happened if Rudy had not been willing to step out into the deep, move to an unfamiliar country, learn a new language and launch his own business with no money all those years ago? I can only wonder.

The greatest legacy I hope we have left for our children and for others is that life is not just about us individually. True life is about others. It's about reaching deep within ourselves to utilize the gifts He has placed within us, and using them to be a blessing for someone else and help unlock the gift within them.

I pray that is the legacy that we will leave for them. And as you read this book, that it is a legacy that will be birthed with you.

—Lavonne Blanco

Part II

AND BEYOND

Chapter 1

IN THE BEGINNING

MY SUMMARY OF "THE BIBLE FOR DUMMIES"
(WHO DON'T WANT TO BE DUMMIES ANYMORE)

I am not a theologian. I'm just a simple guy who wants to understand as much as possible about who God is and what He is telling us in His Word. This summary of the Bible is what I see after reading it from beginning to end five times over the past twenty-five years. I have been reading and studying it and asking God for His revelation regarding what is written.

I am really excited about sharing this with you because it all makes sense to me now. None of this made sense to me before. But now I can see how God is so good to us and wants to hang out in close relationship with each and every one of us.

I know He is real as you can read in the first part of this book. I have experienced His guiding hand on my life, and no one can take that away from me.

In summary, I can tell you that the Bible is a love story. It reveals the never-ending love that God has for His creation and demonstrates over and over the desire God has to hang out with you and me—His creation.

Are you satisfied with the path your life is currently on? If so, then what I'm about to show you can boost wisdom and insight to continue on that path with confidence. But if you are not completely satisfied with the current trajectory of your life, be encouraged, for it can change for the better. While the past cannot be undone, your future has yet to be written. You have unique gifts and talents within you to fulfill a specific destiny. The Bible tells us that God has a plan for each of our lives,

> *"For I know the plans I have for you," declares the Lord, "plans to prosper you and not to harm you, plans to give you hope and a future. Then you will call on me and come and pray to me, and I will listen to you. You will seek me and find me when you seek me with all your heart."[10]*

I can make the decision right now to trust God or not to trust God. I can ask for His help, or choose to run the course of my life on my own. But whether I like it or not, I live with the consequences of my past decisions. Even when I choose not to make a decision, I have in essence made a decision. I see this as we go to the story of the first couple in the Bible, Adam and Eve. It begins with Genesis, the first book of the Bible. And it is here that I can begin to understand so much about God, His heart, His love for us and His purpose for us by examining what happened in the first days of creation.

As you read this, if it is your first time to read through the Bible, may I insert that initially it made very little sense to me when I read it the first time through. It seemed to be bits and pieces of stories that didn't seem connected and were hard to follow, but the more I read it, the more He kept saying to me, "Do you get it now? Do you understand My purpose and My goal?" God encourages us throughout the Bible to meditate on it, and I can see the reason why. It is hard to get it the first time. Now I am convinced that God created us because He wanted to hang out with us. In essence, the Bible is a story about love and relationship.

According to Genesis 1, the Lord God created man and put him in the Garden of Eden to work it and take care of it. Adam and Eve were given a gift in the Garden of Eden. Everything they needed was provided for them in that place. When I understand what happened in the Garden of Eden, I can understand so much about God, His heart, His purpose and why we face so many challenges in the world today. It all started there.

After God made man, He placed him in the Garden to work it and take care of it. So here I see that work is not a bad thing. In fact, work is a good thing. It gives me purpose, and it was created to give me satisfaction. It is a gift I should embrace.

I enjoy the work I do so much that if my wife doesn't call me to come home, I may miss dinner! And I get a kick when someone asks me if a trip I am taking is for work or for pleasure. I can't help but ask, "What do you mean? Work is supposed to be a pleasure!" I get funny looks in return most of the time from that response. But the point I am trying to make is that work was never intended to be a curse.

God created the Garden so that Adam and Eve had everything they needed. A beautiful place that was pleasing to the eye and with plenty of food. They had each other for companionship, and they had a personal relationship with God. Adam also had dominion over all the animals of the earth, so they lived in safety and harmony with their surroundings. Everything was just the way God wanted it to be.

In the Garden, Adam and Eve were given complete freedom...well, almost. They could do whatever they wanted with one simple directive: *"You must not eat from the tree of the knowledge of good and evil, for when you eat from it you will certainly die."*[11] My question is, "Why did God put something there that He didn't want them to eat from? Why include it at all?" This is an important question, because this is where I begin to understand the heart of God.

You see, that directive was for their protection rather than as a restriction. God wanted to protect them from the knowledge of evil. God knew and desired to protect them, but God gave them what He gives to all of us—the power of choice. It is important to note that He always provides us the opportunity to choose.

Unfortunately, Adam and Eve made a poor choice when they chose to disobey, and all of mankind—including you and me—have been paying a price for that choice ever since.

> *Now the serpent was more crafty than any of the wild animals the Lord God had made. He said to the woman, "Did God really say, 'You must not eat from any tree in the garden'?"*
>
> *The woman said to the serpent, "We may eat fruit from the trees in the garden, but God did say, 'You must not eat fruit from the tree that is in the middle of the garden, and you must not touch it, or you will die.'"*
>
> *"You will not certainly die," the serpent said to the woman. "For God knows that whn you eat from it your eyes will be opened, and you will be like God, knowing good and evil."*
>
> *When the woman saw that the fruit of the tree was good for food and pleasing to the eye, and also desirable for gaining wisdom, she took some and ate it. She also gave some to her husband, who was with her, and he ate it. Then the eyes of both of them were opened, and they realized they were naked; so they sewed fig leaves together and made coverings for themselves.*[12]

They chose to disobey God after listening and having a conversation with the serpent which God also created. The serpent was very crafty, because during the conversation with Eve it put just enough doubt in her mind to sway her decision to do what God said not to do.

This is where we have the first connection of evil and death. The two are related and evil will ultimately bring death. When Adam and Eve chose to listen to the serpent and disobey God, their eyes were opened to understand shame, disobedience and evil. Immediately after eating of the fruit, their relationship with God changed and they hid themselves.

God created Adam and Eve to have fellowship with them. We know that because He created them in His image. Each day He went to the Garden to be with them and talk with them. It wasn't in working the Garden or naming the animals they drew close to God. It was in spending time with Him. And that was God's desire to spend time with them.

There is no indication when we read this story that Adam and Eve had any previous intention of disobeying God. But when the serpent came he put pressure on Eve first. "Did God really say, 'You must not eat from any tree in the garden?'" he asked Eve.

Eve's answer was not entirely accurate when she replied, for she added that they must not eat or touch the fruit from the tree that was in the middle of the Garden. If we go back and look at it, God said not to eat of it. He didn't say not to touch it. Where did that come from? She was obviously aware of what God had told Adam. Perhaps Adam added that when he told her of the command. I don't know. What I do know is that external pressure was applied to Eve to question the validity of what God said. As a result, both Adam and Eve disobeyed. They chose to believe the external voice and actions which called into question the commands and purpose of God.

In the center of the Garden, God placed two special trees—the Tree of Life and the Tree of the Knowledge of Good and Evil. *The Lord God made all kinds of trees grow out of the ground—trees that were pleasing to the eye and good for food. In the middle of the garden were the tree of life and the tree of the knowledge of good and evil.*[13] Have you ever wondered why God put those two trees in the Garden in the first place? Or why did He put one, which they were not supposed to eat from, right in the center of the Garden to be a temptation for them? And why did they need a Tree of Life if they could eat from all the other trees?

153

The answer to the last question is found in Genesis 3:22: *"And the Lord God said, 'The man has now become like one of us, knowing good and evil. He must not be allowed to reach out his hand and take also from the tree of life and eat, and live forever.'"*

The fruit from the Tree of Life was what would sustain them forever. Most likely, they would have gone to it frequently for food and life and in doing so would have had to look at the Tree of the Knowledge of Good and Evil which was next to it. Each time they came to eat from the Tree of Life, they would have had to make the decision not to eat from the Tree of the Knowledge of Good and Evil. The decision to be obedient to God's command was not a single decision that occurred just once, but it was a constant decision.

I face the same thing in my life today. I have choices to make each day that will determine the course of my life. I can choose from the "tree of life" with decisions that will bring life or I can choose other fruit, some which will produce death. The Internet is a great example of this which most of us face every day. For in using the Internet we are bombarded with all sorts of temptations that are just a click away. Like Eve, it is easy to rationalize and say, "It will not harm me. If I 'eat' of it, I will not die." But in the end there are always consequences for our actions; and just like Adam and Eve, I have two choices when I face any temptation—to run from it or to partake of it. But the more I fellowship (spend time with) and know God, the easier it is to make the right decision.

I think it's important to note that God didn't intervene during the time the serpent worked to convince Eve to disobey God. Remember, God created the serpent. He could have killed it, made it disappear, or stopped it before it tempted Eve. But He didn't. When she reached up to grab of the fruit, even then He still could have stopped her. Finally, as she took the fruit to share it with Adam, once again He could have intervened, but He did not. This shows us so much about the nature of God. He wants us to choose Him and to choose to obey Him. It is a relationship based on choice. He will not force us to make that decision. He wanted to see what

Adam and Eve would do independently. And independently, they chose to disobey, and so together they lost out on the closeness of the relationship they had with Him. They were removed from the Garden by their choices.

It's important that we look further at how these choices have guided history and how our choices guide our lives.

Chapter 2

CHOICES

God gave us the gift of free choice. Notice that after Adam and Eve disobeyed, God did not suddenly decide to get rid of them and go back to the drawing board to tweak His design. No, God decided to live with the consequences of what He had created, even though it wasn't what He would have chosen, He allowed them to choose even if it wasn't *His* choice.

THE ENTRANCE OF DEATH AND EVIL

So what actually happened when Adam and Eve disobeyed? They were instructed that if they ate of the forbidden fruit they would die. But obviously physical death didn't happen...at least not right away. What did happen was spiritual death in the sense that the relationship they had with God was severed. There is now a separation in their relationship with Him. Their closeness with Him died. They could still talk with Him, but now sin and evil separated them from their relationship with God.

One thing I learned from this is that when I don't have fellowship with God, in His eyes it is like being dead. When I choose to live my life separate from God, I am just going through the motions and missing out on the blessings that God intended for our lives. It is when I fellowship with Him that I truly come alive.

Perhaps that may sound cruel or crazy. But when I think about it, isn't the fact that God gave them a choice true love? If someone says, "If you don't want to love me, then I release you," then that is true love.

Two Kingdoms

When God created the earth, there was only one kingdom—God's Kingdom. It was God and His creation. Man was living inside this Kingdom with no knowledge of evil. That is how God designed it. But when Adam and Eve disobeyed, another kingdom began in which God was not the king. This new kingdom is the world's kingdom, ruled by evil. This is where you and I live, not by God's choice but by man's choice. In this second kingdom, evil exists and mankind has too often allowed this evil to influence his thinking and actions. The evil we face in this world was never part of what God wanted us to experience—it was man's choice that opened the door for evil to rule in the world.

When I was born in this earth, I didn't have a choice. I was born into this world's kingdom and introduced to evil. Just like everyone else, while I had no choice as to what kingdom I was born into, I have complete choice for my personal life and in which kingdom to remain. I can accept God, renew relationship with Him and live with Him forever or remain as I am in this world of evil. I can make the choice to live in God's Kingdom simply by my own decision.

Although Adam and Eve made a decision that separated them and us from God, He later established a plan that would make a way to allow us back to His Kingdom and blessings. Jesus Christ said, *"Very trulyI tell you,,*

158

whoever hears my word and believes him who sent me has eternal life and will not be judged but has crossed over from death to life."[14]

In other words, what this means is that when I believe in Jesus Christ, we move from being dead (spiritually) to being alive, because it is then that I start my relationship and fellowship with God.

THE FORCE OF EVIL

What is evil anyway? I believe it is anything that draws me away from God and His purpose for my life. As I saw with Eve in the Garden, evil will always come to make me doubt God, who I am and my purpose. It will attempt to trick me into pride and the thought that I can handle everything on my own apart from God. It tries to make me believe that if He really loved me, He wouldn't allow evil to exist. But I have to remember, it was invited to exist through man's decision. Yet God has provided a way of escape. It is simply up to me and what choice I make. So what will you choose?

The good news is, I have a choice to enter back into His Kingdom. He made it easy. All I have to do is to believe in Him and choose Him to be my God to enter back into that relationship with Him. So when that external pressure comes just like the serpent came to Eve to make me doubt that God exists, or that He loves me or that He is a good God, the question is, who am I going to listen to?

GOD'S ORIGINAL PLAN WAS FOR BLESSING

"God blessed them and said to them, 'Be fruitful and increase in number; fill the earth and subdue it. Rule over the fish in the sea and the birds in the sky and over every living creature that moves on the ground."[15]

It's important to understand that God's original intent was that man would live in the Garden forever partaking of the good fruit and fellowshipping with Him. He provided for everything. His blessing was without an expiration date. So as we read the very beginning in the first three chapters of the Bible, this is my quick overview about God's original plan.

GOD'S ORIGINAL PLAN

1. God created the earth and all the living plants and animals and said it was good.

2. He created man in His own image.

3. He gave man dominion over all the animals of the earth.

4. He created all kinds of trees with fruit that was good to eat and pleasant to the eye.

5. He created a special tree called the Tree of Life for mankind to eat and live on the earth forever without the knowledge of good and evil.

6. God wanted to have an eternal relationship with man where death does not exist and man is unaware of evil.

7. God created another tree called the Knowledge of Good and Evil which He commanded man not to eat from it. Yet, if they choose to disobey, there are consequences—in this case, that meant that they would die. With this single command God gives man the option to choose to obey Him and live in fellowship with Him or disobey Him and die. Death means a life separated from God.

8. While the Tree of the Knowledge of Good and Evil was available to mankind, God did not want them to partake of it. He never wanted them to be introduced to evil or have knowledge of evil.

9. After God created man, He realized it was not good for man to be alone, so he created another human being called woman using flesh from man.

CHOICES

10. God created woman for man so that together they form a perfect unity. For this reason a man shall leave his father and his mother and be joined to his wife, and they shall become one flesh. This tells me that one man and one woman is what God designed to populate the earth.

11. God said to the man and the woman to fill the earth and to subdue it. This command lets me know that God, who created the earth, is not concerned about overpopulation or its effects.

12. God asked man to work the ground and take care of it. Man has something to do. He is not supposed to sit back idle.

Understanding the Nature of God

It is important to grasp these concepts from the beginning, and it is how I understand the heart and nature of God. God is a good God. He created man and then He created the Garden full of good things for man. He provided plenty of food to eat, a place to live, something to do and a woman to accompany him and be in complete unity with him. Mankind had a personal relationship with God. He knew God and had access to Him.

God put man into a leadership position and provided things for him to do and to take care of, and in doing all of that He provided him with the power of choice. Remember, God never wanted us to choose to know good and evil. Through one man's disobedience evil entered the world. God never wanted that for man from the beginning, and He does not want it for man today. That is where we encounter God's grace.

161

Chapter 3

RELIGION VS. GRACE

When I was young what I understood about "religion" during my school-age years was pretty simple:

1. Don't kill anyone.

2. Don't steal too much.

3. Don't make some big problem, but if I do be ready to recite a prayer dozens of times.

When it boils down to it, I suppose all I really thought of religion at that time was a set of rules. I think for most people who don't have a relationship with God, that is how religion appears—a set of rules we must follow. Yet I had glimpses, even in those early years, that I was somehow missing it. In my heart, I instinctively believed there was something greater and more powerful behind everything—a "Someone" rather than just something.

Time and again, when I was in trouble I would call out to that "Someone" for deliverance...and deliverance came. I saw that deliverance even

163

in something as simple as a spanking. As a child when I knew I had one coming, I would get down on my knees and with a sincere heart make a petition, "God, can You save me from this? I won't do it again if You will save me." Interestingly, each time His supernatural hand delivered me. Through those experiences, I learned something important. I knew I could run to Him when I was consciously repentant of a wrongdoing and He would deliver me. That is called the faith of a child, but the truth of it stuck with me. There was a God, and He heard my prayers. Still, it would take years before I really tried to get to know Him further.

God's grace means favor we don't deserve. Mercy provides deliverance when we deserve punishment. I remember one specific incident that really demonstrates what happens when we make a poor choice. It is what grace is all about.

In elementary school I liked to run. In fact, I was one of the fastest runners in the class in third grade. I figured that out when we would play games at recess, and I can remember running either a race or in a game of some kind and the other kids could not catch up to me.

During our break time at school, we would go out to the patio and play "Quedó," better known in English as "Tag." If you run fast, you are never "it." I was rarely "it."

One day, the principal of our school came into the classroom and instructed us that there was to be no more running in the halls. I'm sure her admonition came partly due to our game. We would be so excited to get out to the playground once the bell rang ending class that we would all run down the hall to make our way to the playground.

Not long after as we sat in class, it was getting close to time for our break. Our group that usually played "Quedó" together determined before the bell rang who would be "it." I sat in my chair watching the clock tick off the remaining minutes and once it sounded, I was off and out the door. I was already focused on watching the kid who was "it" so I wouldn't get tagged! I started sprinting down the hall when I turned to find him. He was already in pursuit of me. Unfortunately, as I kept my eyes on him, I didn't notice that a teacher was walking out of her classroom with her arms full of books. I plowed straight into her. She went flying as did her books. It laid her out on the ground. I apologized profusely as I ran around and picked up all of her books. I helped her stand and handed the books back to her, but she was furious.

"The principal is going to hear about this, young man!" she exclaimed, her face flushed with anger.

I knew I was in big trouble. Because once I got in trouble at school, a spanking at home was sure to follow.

My mom was the disciplinarian in our family, and she didn't mess around. With four boys and three girls, she didn't let things get out of control and was quick to follow through with punishment. "Bring me the belt," were the words my siblings and I dreaded, because we knew Mom meant what she said. With the threat of the teacher still ringing in my ears, I knew I was going to hear those words from my mom again.

While my mom was a staunch advocate for discipline, the funny thing was she wouldn't get upset about my grades if they were low in regular core subjects. However, if the grade I received in Conducta or "Behavior" was anything but an "A," there would definitely be discipline in store. I knew this fiasco of running over the teacher would ruin my grade in Conducta. "I'm sooo in trouble," I thought to myself.

Later that day, the principal walked into our classroom. My heart sunk as she called out, "Where is Rodolfo Blanco?" As if their heads were all attached to a machine, all of my classmates turned and looked at me. It was evident by her tone that I was about to get it. And get it I did. For the next several minutes she let me have it right in front of my classmates. When she was finished chewing me out, she handed me a letter. "Give this to your mother. She will have to sign it before you can return to class."

That letter felt like a one-hundred pound weight in my pocket. On my way home I read the principal's note detailing what had happened that day. I shuddered knowing it was an automatic spanking.

Once home I pulled out the letter and reread it, noting the space for my mother's name and signature. My mind began to whirl. Was there any option of how to escape the inevitable? That's when I had an idea. I searched for a pen and paper and walked into the kitchen where my mother was working. "How do you sign your name?" I asked as I put the pen and paper down in front of her. To my amazement she signed it and handed it back to me. I took that paper and practiced signing her name over and over until I could copy it pretty closely. Finally, I took out the note from the principal, signed it, folded it back up and took it to school.

I thought I was so smart and had worked my way out of that punishment. I handed the letter to the principal the next day and thought it was over. But about a week later it was time for parent-teacher conferences. This is when the parents go to the school to receive the grade cards for their student and meet with the principal and teachers. Oh no! It dawned on me that when my mom went to talk with the teacher they would hand her the folder that would include not only my grades, but the letter of Conducta in which I had faked her signature.

I got down on my knees in desperation and prayed, "Oh God, deliver me from this. If You will, I promise You, *promise You*, that I will never ever forge my mom's signature again." I was so completely repentant. But I also knew I could do nothing to change the outcome.

Prior to that time, my mom had never missed a parent-teacher conference. Never. But that morning when it came time for her to go she pulled me aside and said, "Rodolfo, tell your teacher I cannot come today." To this day I can't remember why she didn't go that day. All I knew was God had intervened on my behalf. To my knowledge my mom never knew of that incident until I told her years later.

So that is an example of mercy. Although I deserved punishment for my poor choice, I was spared punishment when I repented and asked God for help. I didn't deserve it, but I received it.

It's important that we realize the importance of this truth. God will grant mercy to us when we repent and choose to receive Him. It's not about what we deserve. I deserved punishment for being disobedient and running the teacher over. But I received mercy and forgiveness even after forging my mom's signature.

That is the very nature of God. It wasn't only that instance that proved this to me. His grace can be seen as we look back through history.

After Adam and Eve disobeyed God, they avoided taking responsibility for their actions, but instead passed the blame. Adam blamed Eve and Eve blamed the serpent. The serpent did not take responsibility either.

This makes me wonder, what would have happened if Adam and Eve instead would have been quick to repent of their disobedience and pleaded for mercy and grace to God?

Chapter 4

A Look Through
History Tells a Story

Each time I read the Bible I gained a better understanding of God, His nature and what He desires for us. But I remember the first time I read through it, it was not clear at all. If you feel that way right now, don't be discouraged. Just as in any relationship, the more time we spend with someone and get to know how they respond, we get to know who they are. So also, the more I read the stories in the Bible and how God responds, the more I clearly understand that He has a heart of love for us. His desire was that we humans would never be introduced to evil. Instead due to choices made by Adam and Eve, evil became a ruler of the world. The first 1500 years of history reveal the effects of those choices.

Because of their choices, Adam and Eve were forced to leave the Garden of Eden and never return. They started on a new journey with the realization now that their choices and actions had consequences. As we continue to read through Genesis and the account of Adam and Eve, we learn they had two sons, Cain and Abel. Like their parents, Cain and Abel had choices to make each day which could result in either good or evil. Unfortunately, their son Cain chose evil.

> *"In the course of time Cain brought some of the fruits of the soil as an offering to the Lord. And Abel also brought an offering—fat portions from some of the firstborn of his flock. The Lord looked with favor on Abel and his offering, but on Cain and his offering he did not look with favor. So Cain was very angry, and his face was downcast."*[16]

> *"Then the Lord said to Cain, 'Why are you angry? Why is your face downcast? If you do what is right, will you not be accepted? But if you do not do what is right, sin is crouching at your door; it desires to have you, but you must rule over it.'"*[8]

> *"Now Cain said to his brother Abel, 'Let's go out to the field.' And while they were in the field, Cain attacked his brother Abel and killed him."*[9]

Jealousy entered into the heart of Cain and as a result, he killed his own brother. The evil that is in the world has now manifested in the form of murder. We see murder repeated just five generations later as Cain's relative Lamech proclaims:

> *"Adah and Zillah, listen to me; wives of Lamech, hear my words. I have killed a man for wounding me, a young man for injuring me."*[17]

So evil continues to spread in the earth as do the actions that come from evil. Here we can see not only murder, but also pride and the decision to take justice into his own hands due to an offense. Violence has become commonplace.

Let's look at how the world has grown to that point: Adam lived to be 930 years old and had other sons and daughters besides Cain and Abel. One-hundred-and-twenty-six years after Adam died, Noah was born. There are nine generations separating Adam and Noah for a total of 1056 years from the time Adam was created to the time Noah was born. We are also told that Adam's third son, Seth, had only been dead fourteen years before Noah was born. It seems hard to believe, but people lived much longer in the early days of biblical history. Yet that was all about to change.

The longer man was on the earth, the more evil grew. Each person had the opportunity every day of their life to choose good or evil. That is a choice we get to make each day as well, and God desires that we choose good.

The pattern and choice for evil had grown so intensely over the first 1500 years until finally the Lord regretted His decision to have created man.

> *"The Lord saw how great the wickedness of the human race had become on the earth, and that every inclination of the thoughts of the human heart was only evil all the time. The Lord regretted that he had made human beings on the earth, and his heart was deeply troubled. So the Lord said, 'I will wipe from the face of the earth the human race I have created—and with them the animals, the birds and the creatures that move along the ground—for I regret that I have made them.' But Noah found favor in the eyes of the Lord (or walked closely with the Lord)."[18]*

Can't you just see God saying, "I knew it! I knew it! That's why I didn't want them to be aware of evil. Look at their condition now!"

It's hard to imagine that God could experience regret and pain from what we do. I mean, isn't He God? But let's look at it from a different vantage point. Are you a parent? If so, you know the pain your heart can experience when your child makes a decision that you know might result in something bad. And yet, they are their own person, and we can't make them make the right decision. Yet, our hearts hurt and are troubled when they experience the consequences of poor decisions. When we can see God as a parent, our Father who created us, and is hurt when we make wrong choices, we can begin to understand His nature better.

171

And just as a parent is hurt when their child chooses to leave or discontinue the relationship with him or her for whatever reason, so it is with God. When we choose to not have relationship with Him, it causes Him pain, and yet He still gives us complete freedom to make that choice.

Where Does Evil Hide Today?

In the Garden of Eden, evil hid in the serpent. We can see this wasn't a normal serpent. Even more interesting, in my opinion, is that Eve doesn't seem surprised that the serpent talked with her. Instead, she has a conversation with a serpent. In my opinion, that was the problem. Why didn't she run to Adam and to God and say, "Hey, a serpent just talked to me like a human, and he told me to eat from the tree that You told us not to eat from. What should I do?" Instead, she had a conversation with the serpent. By allowing the conversation to continue, the serpent was able to plant seeds of doubt in Eve's mind which took hold. She didn't run from the temptation to do what she was told not to do. Instead, she allowed herself to be talked into the very thing that would destroy their idyllic lives and relationship they had with God. It was a trap, and she walked right into it.

It's no different today. Evil is present and it speaks to us through people, the media and various aspects of daily life. It will almost always try to speak to us when we are alone and isolated from family and friends who would help us recognize what is happening and speak wisdom to us. And when we choose to entertain the conversation and thoughts contrary to what we know to be right, then it begins to look good and sound reasonable at least for the moment. Yet the result is destruction to our lives.

If we can begin to recognize this pattern, then maybe we will be smarter and avoid the tragic mistake that Eve made. Evil will always seek a place of entry into our lives. This mostly comes from what we allow entrance into our lives. The television is an example. The "surprise factor" of a metal and plastic box talking to us (where a serpent talking to Eve should have been a surprise factor) is no longer present. We accept it and with it whatever pours from it almost without exception. And so all evil has to do is plant a thought in our minds so that we will question God's purpose and plan. We see this in some television shows, which work really hard at redefining good and evil, or redefining the definition of love. It's the same old trick of deception used from the beginning of time.

"Then the Lord God said to the woman, 'What is this you have done?' The woman said, 'The serpent deceived me, and I ate.'"[19] Eve recognized this deception after she had disobeyed God. But it was too late by then.

Another place where evil resides is in our schools, colleges and universities. When a professor begins to plant thoughts into a student's mind that God does not exist, or that He doesn't really mean what He says, or that the Bible is not the Word of God, then it is the same as the serpent in days of old. I'm not saying that every television program, movie, talk show, professor or teacher is evil. Not at all. What I am saying is that we have to recognize that there is a strategy from evil to cause us to doubt God and separate us from Him. Evil wants to destroy our lives, and it has done a good job at it.

It is also important to note that evil pursued Eve first rather than Adam. This was a strategy in which evil determined it had a better chance approaching the woman first. And it worked. We see this in our society today where the role of men has been minimized. From the beginning, man was to fill the role of protector as a father and a husband for the family. When the culture continually portrays the father/husband as a weak leader, or on the contrary, a dictator, it weakens the integrity of the family unity. When the family disintegrates and the children and wife question the heart and motives of the father, that is another victory for evil. Isn't this what we see has happened in our world today?

Just like in the Garden when the serpent called into question the wisdom of God—evil continues to seek to destroy the relationships of families and to devalue the role of the father in the home . It is time to wake up.

173

Chapter 5

A Time to Start Over

So what happened during the first 1500 years of mankind when they lived with no rules all doing what each man saw fit? Nothing good. Evil filled the earth, *"Now the earth was corrupt in God's sight and was full of violence. God saw how corrupt the earth had become, for all the people on earth had corrupted their ways."*[20]

I don't know exactly what the people were doing that corrupted God's ways, but what I do know is that evil had overtaken the land. The definition of the word "corruption" is:

- dishonest or illegal behavior especially by powerful people (such as government officials or police officers);

- the act of corrupting someone or something;

- something that has been changed from its original form.[21]

Corruption is a departure from the original intent of what is pure or correct. So the people obviously moved away in their behavior and choices from God's original intent of what was pure and right. (Isn't this similar to what we see in the world today?) What I believe we can see from this look in history is that evil has the power to completely detour us from what is good and peaceful and from the destiny God has for us.

As was true in the Garden of Eden, so it is 1500 years later, man's decision to choose evil over good created his destiny. As God looked out over the world He created, a world that had become consumed with violence and corruption, He saw only one man who had chosen good over evil. One. This is the account of Noah and his family.

"Noah was a righteous man, blameless among the people of his time, and he walked faithfully with God."[22]

Noah walked with God. And so God chose to destroy every living creature and instructed Noah to start over again in hopes that mankind would return to Him. While that may sound harsh and unfair, this is where it is important that we begin to understand the nature of God. He created us to walk with Him in holiness and goodness. It is His nature.

Can you imagine the conversation between Noah and God at that time? When God said to Noah, *"I am going to bring floodwaters on the earth to destroy all life under the heavens, every creature that has the breath of life in it. Everything on earth will perish."*[23] I can picture Noah maybe a little nervous asking God, "Did You say You were going to destroy all the people? All of them? Including me and my family?"

To Noah's comfort God said, *"But I will establish my covenant with you, and you will enter the ark—you and your sons and your wife and your sons' wives with you."*[24]

God told Noah to build a boat—an ark—big enough for his family and two of each kind of animal to preserve their race. Everything else would be destroyed in the flood. And while that may sound like a harsh punishment, it is important to realize that it took Noah one hundred years to build the ark. One hundred years for the people of that day to come up to him and ask what he was doing in which they would have received a warning of the impending judgment upon the human race. One hundred years that they could have repented and changed their ways. That's because God is patient. He wanted to give them ample opportunity to change. But they didn't.

The name of Noah's grandfather, Methuselah, gives us insight into one way God speaks and the extent of His patience and mercy. The name Methusaleh means "when he is dead it shall be sent."[25] Methuselah was 187 years old when he had Lamech, Noah's father. Lamech was 182 years old when he had Noah. Noah was 600 years old when the floodwaters came upon the earth. That would have made Methuselah—the oldest man to have ever lived—969 years old at the time of the flood. Noah's father, Lamech, died five years before the flood took place and would have watched his son build the ark for ninety-five years. Methusaleh died just before the flood takes place. So during the entire life of Methusaleh, God was giving the people a chance to change and repent of their evil. Methusaleh lived longer than any other man. I believe God extended His life in His patience just waiting to see if change would come. But it did not. So when Methusaleh died it was sent. What was sent? The flood.

We can look at Noah's family and see that he came from a long line that honored God. His great-grandfather, Enoch, was a man who chose good over evil, for the Bible says of him that Enoch lived 365 years and he walked with God the last 300 years after his son Methusaleh was born. He did not die, but God took him to be with Him. This was not a punishment, but an honor for one who chose to walk in fellowship with Him. The people of the earth at that time knew that. It was part of their history, but unfortunately there were very few who made that choice.

Noah continued that family line in honoring God. He built the ark to God's specific instructions. It is recorded that it took approximately one hundred years. Once he was done, God brought all kinds of pairs of animals, male and female, to the ark. God instructed Noah to get enough food and water for his wife, sons and his sons' wives and animals to last forty days and forty nights during which time the earth would be flooded with water.

Noah, his family and the animals entered the boat, God shut the door and it began to rain. After they emerged from the ark, Noah's first act was to honor God, and God made a promise to him that He would never completely flood the earth again. His seal of that promise shows up in the rainbow which He set in the sky as a reminder of that promise.

> *"I establish my covenant with you: Never again will all life be destroyed by the waters of a flood; never again will there be a flood to destroy the earth." And God said, "This is the sign (visible symbol, memorial) of the covenant I am making between me and you and every living creature that is with you, a covenant for all generations to come; I have set my rainbow in the clouds, and it will be the sign of the covenant between me and the earth."*[26]

As you read this, do you feel that God's actions to destroy mankind with the flood were unfair and unjust? That those who died in the flood had no opportunity to change or ask for forgiveness? What you will read next is an amazing indicator of God's nature which is found in the New Testament in 1 Peter 3:18-20 which says:

> *"For Christ also has once suffered for sins, the just for the unjust, so that He might bring us to God, being put to death in the flesh, but made alive by the Spirit, by whom He also went and preached to the spirits in prison, who in times past were disobedient, when God waited patiently in the days of Noah while the ark was being prepared."*[27]

This reveals to me that God is just and fair and reconfirms His patience toward man. For those who were disobedient while Noah was building the ark and died in the flood, God provided another opportunity to be reconciled with Him. Although their bodies died physically, their spirits were still alive—just imprisoned for about 2000 years. After Jesus died on the cross, He went and preached to those who had disobeyed long ago, and

He provided them another opportunity—the opportunity to be reconciled with God for the forgiveness of their sins.

What did Jesus Christ preach to them when He went to where they were? It is logical to think He preached the same thing to them that He preached when He was here on the earth. That if they would believe and accept Him as the Son of God, then they could enter back into fellowship and relationship with God their Creator. All the people who died during the flood had a second chance. Why? Because that is His nature. God is just and fair. And He desires that everyone comes back to relationship with Him.

Can you see that pattern as you follow this history? This is God's plan on how to defeat evil. It is to make a way for everyone to choose what is right and to have a second chance. This still applies today.

Once the flood ended, Noah and his family began to repopulate the earth again as we see in Genesis 9:19: *"These were the three sons of Noah, and from them came the people who were scattered over the whole earth."* And although the world is essentially starting over fresh, evil is a spiritual thing that manifests through physical beings. And so while the evil people were destroyed, evil is still lurking, ready to take up residence again in those who will allow it a place.

At this point, God sets up some new, specific rules relating to the value of human life. *"And for your lifeblood I will surely demand an accounting. I will demand an accounting from every animal. And from each human being, too, I will demand an accounting for the life of another human being."*[28]

God was aware how violent man could be after observing man's first 1500 years living without any specific rules of behavior; and yet evil begins to influence mankind's behavior again despite making man accountable for another person's death.

179

Noah lived 350 years after the flood for a total of 950 years. He lived to see ten more generations born after the flood. During that same time, God tries another plan to establish His Kingdom on earth.

Chapter 6

GOD TRIES TO ESTABLISH HIS KINGDOM ON EARTH AGAIN

It had been approximately 2024 years since the time of Adam and Eve and approximately 368 years since the flood. Noah had been dead approximately eighteen years. God's desire remains the same. He desires to have relationship with mankind. He relentlessly pursues that relationship and continues to try to make a way to reestablish His blessings.

At this point, God chose a seventy-five-year-old man named Abram from the land of Ur and said to him, *"I will make you into a great nation, and I will bless you; I will make your name great, and you will be a blessing. I will bless those who bless you, and whoever curses you I will curse; and all peoples on earth will be blessed through you."*[29]

Obviously, God is thinking of implementing a plan to bless one man and through him all people on earth. It is interesting to consider that Noah and Abram could have met, for after Abram was born, Noah still lived another fifty-seven years. The time span of mankind changed after the flood. Before the flood, the Lord said, *"My Spirit will not contend with humans forever, for they are mortal; their days will be a hundred and twenty years."*[30] Noah lived 950 years, but Abram (later renamed Abraham) lived 175 years. It is evident that the life span of man became shorter and shorter until what we know today. We can see how evil changed the original plan. That's what evil does even today. It corrupts God's plan for mankind.

There are eleven times in the book of Genesis in which God repeats His desire to bless Abraham and his descendants so they can be a blessing to other nations. This provides an opportunity to see once again how God made a plan to bless all of us through Abraham. Here is a list of the times He repeats those blessings:

1. *"I will make you into a great nation, and I will bless you; I will make your name great, and you will be a blessing. I will bless those who bless you, and whoever curses you I will curse; and all peoples on earth will be blessed through you."*[31]

This is the first time God speaks this to Abram (Abraham). At that time Abraham was seventy-five years old and Sarai, his wife, was sixty-five—too old to have children, and yet God has told him He will make him a father of many nations. It will take a miracle to accomplish this promise. It shows once again God's desire to have relationship with humans and a plan for it to happen.

2. *"The Lord appeared to Abram and said, 'To your offspring I will give this land.' So he built an altar there to the Lord, who had appeared to him."*[32] God confirms to Abram that he will have children.

3. After some years passed, although *"Abram had become very wealthy in livestock and in silver and gold"*[33] he had no children yet. It would be easy for Abraham to doubt the promise he received. So once

again God confirms to him that he will have children—many children—and the land the Lord will provide for them when He tells him, *"All the land that you see I will give to you and your offspring forever."*[34]

As God is building this new Kingdom on earth through Abram, evil is hard at work bringing sin and corruption among other people in the land.

"Now the people of Sodom were wicked and were sinning greatly against the Lord."[35]

4. Sometime later, God continues to confirm His message to Abraham: *"He took him outside and said, 'Look up at the sky and count the stars—if indeed you can count them.' Then he said to him, 'So shall your offspring be.'"*[36]

This is the fourth time this promise is repeated to Abram, and finally he believes it. At this time there is something else going on with a group of people called the Amorites. God tells Abraham, *"In the fourth generation your descendants will come back here, for the sin of the Amorites has not yet reached its full measure."*[37]

From that statement it appears that God sees ahead the evil that is taking place through the Amorites and lets Abraham know that it's just a matter of time before destruction will come to them because of their sin.

God also warns him that his descendants will become slaves in a land for 400 years. That land is Egypt.

When I read this it makes me wonder, why does God allow this to happen? If He wants to bless Abraham and his descendants, then couldn't He have prevented this slavery and abuse? I asked God about that several times. I couldn't understand why God would allow it to happen. But even this has a purpose, for it allows the people to see their need for God and to recognize that they are unable to save themselves from this oppression. During the time of slavery, they didn't have the time or ability to indulge in sin and go their own way as the Egyptians did who enslaved them.

Instead, they cried out to God. It brought them to a place of purification in themselves as they looked to Him. And when God rescued them, He did it big and in such a meaningful way that it is a continual reminder for them of His power and love for them.

> *"And I have promised to bring you up out of your misery in Egypt into the land of the Canaanites, Hittites, Amorites, Perizzites, Hivites and Jebusites—a land flowing with milk and honey."*[38]

> *"And God spoke all these words: 'I am the Lord your God, who brought you out of Egypt, out of the land of slavery.'"*[39]

> *"Then I will dwell among the Israelites and be their God."*[40]

God is still in the rescuing business today. It is His nature which we can see over and over. His desire is to bless and to deliver. But as we can see, even as early as back in the Garden of Eden, He also allowed us a choice. That's why there were *two* trees in the Garden of Eden. Adam and Eve were given a choice whether to follow His commands or not. It has always been God's nature to allow humanity to have a choice. The direction we choose and the results are our choice.

I have seen this in my own life on numerous occasions and have seen the goodness and power of God supernaturally provide for me and my family, and how He has delivered me from difficult situations and enabled me to start my own business when it looked impossible. Yet it was also up to me to make choices that would enable those blessings. The best choice I believe I had was to run *to* God and not *away* from God. Even when running to God is hard, He helps us make the right choice.

5. God once again confirms this promise: *"On that day the Lord made a covenant with Abram and said, 'To your descendants I give this land, from the Wadi of Egypt to the great river, the Euphrates.'"*[41]

Now ten years have passed and still Abraham and Sarah are childless. So they began to make their own plan on how to speed things up. That's normally when we get into trouble when we divert from God's plan to

184

make our own. Eve did this and we see the results. Sarah, since she hadn't yet conceived, made a plan on how to have a child through her servant. It was ill conceived and caused problems as she and Abraham began to work their plan rather than God's. And yet, He allowed them to make their own choices.

So, in trying to cause God's plan to come about, Abraham had a child with Sarah's servant. But this was their plan, not God's plan. It is important that we understand that when we try to bring God's plan about in our way and timing, it will always create problems. This happened to Abraham and Sarah when they tried to force God's plan to come in *their* timing, which then created a bigger complication in their home. After Sarai (Sarah's name before God changed it) took her maidservant, Hagar, and gave her to Abraham to sleep with, the maidservant conceived a child. And now as the one who produced an heir for Abraham, she despised Sarai. Sarai's pain multiplied and she blames Abraham for her suffering. To compensate, Abraham tells Sarai to do whatever she thinks is best with her maidservant. And so Sarai pays Hagar back with the same treatment which she received from her maidservant. Eventually under such mistreatment, Hagar and her son flee into the desert.[42] Look at the mess Abraham and Sarai find themselves in, not to mention the pain it caused Hagar.

6. Finally, about fourteen years later, when Abraham was ninety-nine years old, God once again confirmed His promise.

"'I will bless her and will surely give you a son by her. I will bless her so that she will be the mother of nations; kings of peoples will come from her.' Abraham fell facedown; he laughed and said to himself, 'Will a son be born to a man a hundred years old? Will Sarah bear a child at the age of ninety?'"[43]

It is interesting to me that the fourth time God spoke this promise to him, Abraham believed what the Lord promised him. God even credited that belief to him as righteousness. However, now I don't see him too convinced of what was promised.

Abram laughed, convinced that it was all just a joke. He tried to talk God into using Ishmael, the son he had fourteen years before, but just as God promised, Abram's wife Sarai conceived. Both of them receive a name change. Abram becomes Abraham, which means "father of many nations;" and Sarai, which meant "quarrelsome," was changed to Sarah which means "princess." It is God's confirmation of what He has promised. *Now the Lord was gracious to Sarah as he had said, and the Lord did for Sarah what he had promised.*[44]

Not only did God bless Abraham and Sarah with a son, Isaac, just as He promised, but Abraham went on to live seventy-five more years and Sarah went on to live another thirty-seven years. Now get this. After his wife, Sarah, died, Abraham married another wife and had six more children with her. All of this was more than forty years after he laughed at the thought of having a child because he was so old.

What did I learn from this? That God will fulfill His promise to us—always. He can do the impossible. And even when I make a mistake and try to "help" God and do it in my own way, as Abraham and Sarah did, God can still set things right and bring about His plan. This is His nature. This is who He is.

7. The seventh confirmation of God's promise to Abraham occurs just before the destruction of the cities of Sodom and Gomorrah. What was the reason for the destruction? Once again, evil was present which prohibited God from establishing His blessing on mankind. Yet, God promised, *"Abraham will surely become a great and powerful nation, and all nations on earth will be blessed through him."*[45] The cities of Sodom and Gomorrah were notable because they were so completely filled with evil.

Now Abram's nephew, Lot, was living in that place. Although God promised He would never destroy the entire world again by flood, these two cities, because of their overwhelming evil, were set to be destroyed.

186

"Now the people of Sodom were wicked and were sinning greatly against the Lord."[46]

Who were these people living in those two cities, and what were they doing to merit that decision?

The people living in Sodom and Gomorrah were descendants of Canaan, the son of Ham, who was the son of Noah. The genealogy of these descendants is as follows: *"Canaan was the father of Sidon his firstborn, and of the Hittites, Jebusites, Amorites, Girgashites, Hivites, Arkites, Sinites, Arvadites, Zemarites and Hamathites."*[47]

There was a curse over the Canaanites because of Canaan's father Ham, *"When Noah awoke from his wine and found out what his youngest son had done to him, he said, 'Cursed be Canaan! The lowest of slaves will he be to his brothers.'"*[48]

Noah spoke a curse over Canaan because of Ham's actions. It is unclear what he did or why it wasn't spoken over Ham, but instead over Noah's grandson; but here is an interesting connection. It is the Canaanites who were the people that inhabited the land of Sodom and Gomorrah, which was overrun with evil. I wonder if this had something to do with the curse.

We are only given a glimpse of the evil that permeated the people of these two cities when God sends two angels to remove Abraham's nephew, Lot, and his family before the destruction takes place.

"The two angels arrived at Sodom in the evening, and Lot was sitting in the gateway of the city. When he saw them, he got up to meet them and bowed down with his face to the ground. 'My lords,' he said, 'please turn aside to your servant's house. You can wash your feet and spend the night and then go on your way early in the morning.'

"'No,' they answered, 'we will spend the night in the square.'

"But he insisted so strongly that they did go with him and entered his house. He prepared a meal for them, baking bread without yeast, and they ate."[49]

Lot doesn't initially recognize that the two men are really angels. When he invites them to come to his home to stay for the night, it's not because he simply wanted to be hospitable. He knows that the city is not safe for strangers. At first the two strangers refuse his offer, but in the end they go with him. Lot offers them a place to lodge and food, but by nightfall, there is trouble.

The men of the city, both young and old, surround Lot's house and begin to pound on his door to demand that Lot send out the two men.

"Before they had gone to bed, all the men from every part of the city of Sodom—both young and old—surrounded the house. They called to Lot, 'Where are the men who came to you tonight? Bring them out to us so that we can have sex with them.'

"Lot went outside to meet them and shut the door behind him and said, 'No, my friends. Don't do this wicked thing.'"[50]

It is clear that what the men of the city wanted to do with the two male strangers was wicked in Lot's eyes. Obviously, the men of the city did not care, for it says that they all came out, young and old alike. Also, in Genesis 13:13 we are told, *"Now the people of Sodom were wicked and were sinning greatly against the Lord."* It is obvious that God was not happy with the behavior of this people to the point He was willing to destroy them.

I can also get additional insight into this situation from another passage: *"In a similar way, Sodom and Gomorrah and the surrounding towns gave themselves up to sexual immorality and perversion. They serve as an example of those who suffer the punishment of eternal fire."*[51]

Just based on these passages, it is easy for me to see a connection between the wicked sins these men were performing such as homosexual acts and immorality and the destruction of the cities where they lived.

So the battle between good and evil never disappeared after the flood. It still existed. And it still involved choice. Sodom and Gomorrah were indeed destroyed by fire raining down from heaven. Their actions had consequences. And yet God's original desire was to bring blessing to people.

8. The eighth confirmation comes with a test. *"Then God said, 'Take your son, your only son, whom you love—Isaac—and go to the region of Moriah. Sacrifice him there as a burnt offering on a mountain I will show you.'"*[52]

Why would God ask Abraham to do this? Remember, God always gives us a choice. This was a choice for Abraham. Was he willing to trust and obey God even when it didn't make sense? Was he willing to give up the one thing for which he so desired? The answer is yes, but God didn't want or plan to kill Isaac. He simply wanted to see Abraham's heart. What was at the throne of Abraham's heart? His son Isaac or God? Remember, God already instructed Abraham that he should have no other gods before Him. When we make people, relationships or things more important than God, we are putting them at the throne of our heart. Abraham, in his willingness to offer up Isaac, was saying, "I trust that even if I sacrifice my son to You that You are well able to raise him up again."

It is also interesting to note in the above verse, that God refers to Isaac as Abraham's "only son." Ishmael is not recognized as a son.

Some may feel it is unfair that God did not recognize Ishmael as a son in that statement. When we take matters into our own hands to bring about a desired result, God isn't obligated to work through our plans. Yet, He did indeed bless Ishmael and made of him a nation. However, it was one of constant struggle because he was birthed out of man's attempt, not God's.

9. The ninth confirmation of this promise was passed to Abraham's son, Isaac, when he was sixty years old and his wife, Rebekah, gave birth to twins Esau and Jacob. *"Stay in this land for a while, and I will be with you and will bless you. For to you and your descendants I*

will give all these lands and will confirm the oath I swore to your father Abraham."[53]

At that time Abraham was 160 years old and God was still confirming His promise only now through Abraham's son. It seems that God had finally found a man who was willing to follow Him and wanted a relationship with Him—something He had not found in Adam.

I believe God is always looking for people willing to listen to His voice and for hearts committed to Him. And when He finds them, His blessings will follow. As Abraham obeyed Him, He wanted his descendants to continue, but as long as there are people living outside of that blessing, God continues to make a way so that they can return to it and fellowship with Him. That has been His plan then and today. It has never changed.

10. The tenth confirmation of the promise to Isaac, Abraham's son, states, *"That night the Lord appeared to him and said, 'I am the God of your father Abraham. Do not be afraid, for I am with you; I will bless you and will increase the number of your descendants for the sake of my servant Abraham.'"*[54] It is important to note that Isaac did not receive the blessing because of anything he had done, but because of what his father, Abraham, had done. What can I learn from this? That one person who will run to God rather than from God, can create a legacy of blessings for his children and grandchildren. That is what I want to do for my children and grandchildren.

11. The eleventh and final confirmation of this promise comes to Abraham's grandson, Jacob. *"There above it stood the Lord, and he said: 'I am the Lord, the God of your father Abraham and the God of Isaac. I will give you and your descendants the land on which you are lying.'"*[55]

After many years passed, Abraham's decendants became the nation of Israel and God fulfilled His promise to them. He continued to show Abraham's descendants that He was faithful to that promise. It was all about creating relationship.

"So the Lord gave Israel all the land he had sworn to give their ancestors, and they took possession of it and settled there."[56]

But while God was there to bless and fulfill His promise, the people of Israel didn't always keep their relationship with Him—and the result turned into disaster as you will see!

Chapter 7

THE PEOPLE CRIED OUT

Why does it seem to take some type of disaster, challenge or lack in our lives to bring us to a place to begin to think about God? And yet, just as it is today, it has always been. Although God was faithful to fulfill His promise to Abraham and make him a father of many nations, once the people of Israel began to prosper, they often forgot about God.

Abraham's grandson, Jacob, went on to have twelve sons who became the twelve founding tribes of the nation of Israel—known as the Jewish or Hebrew nation. And his children and children's children were very blessed. But that didn't mean that it was always easy. There were trials and challenges they faced, just as we face challenges today.

For example, the fourth time God spoke His promise to Abraham, He also said, *"Then the Lord said to him, 'Know for certain that for four hundred years your descendants will be strangers in a country not their own and that they will be enslaved and mistreated there.*"[57]

Abraham's descendants grew and prospered and were blessed. But eventually due to a famine in the land, many of Abraham's descendants through the line of Abraham's grandson, Jacob, relocated to Egypt where Abraham's great-grandson, Joseph, had been promoted to a position of leadership, just second under the king of the land. Talk about a blessing. But eventually after Joseph died and time had passed, the favor that had been upon the Hebrew people living in Egypt was gone and the Egyptians turned them into slaves for the next 400 years, thus fulfilling the scriptural prophecy given in the previous paragraph.

For some time I struggled with the question of why God would make Abraham's descendants go through that kind of oppression. What was the purpose for their becoming slaves for such a long time? And if God knew they were going to be slaves, why didn't He do something to prevent it?

He had provided for them during the time of famine, but after it was over and their needs met, their heart had grown distant...and so had their good relationship with the Egyptians who now forced them into slavery, but God once again came to rescue them.

> *"During that long period, the king of Egypt died. The Israelites groaned in their slavery and cried out, and their cry for help because of their slavery went up to God. God heard their groaning and he remembered his covenant with Abraham, with Isaac and with Jacob. So God looked on the Israelites and was concerned about them."*[58]

The Israelites had served as slaves for 400 long years in Egypt and as they cried out to God, He responded. But my question was, "Why didn't He jump in to rescue them before that? Why did He even let them go into slavery?" One morning I woke up and felt I had my answer from God to this question, and it was all about relationship.

194

Remember, He always allows us a choice. If I choose to remove Him from my life, then He will honor my decision, even if it is not what He desires. When I consider this, it seems clear that I often create my own challenges. I can track back through history where I see Adam and Eve disobeyed Him and therefore completely messed up His original plan. Even though Abraham didn't fully understand and tried to make things happen his own way, he ultimately chose to trust, obey and honor the relationship. As a result, God set about to bless Abraham and his descendants and to bring about recovery and relationship for the entire human race.

Through Abraham's grandson, Jacob, we see the plan taking form as twelve tribes are formed from his descendants. Twelve represents government or kingdom, and it is from these twelve that He wants to establish His Kingdom. When Jacob and his family moved to Egypt, they totaled about seventy people. It was an unlikely journey, one only God could have orchestrated as we see a Hebrew rise to such a level of leadership in the Egyptian government. Joseph's installation in that position saved Abraham's descendants from starvation and death as famine struck the land. Abraham's descendants remained in Egypt for the next 430 years. They multiplied from seventy to around 600,000 men and that wasn't counting women and children, which would have brought the number close to two million. The Israelites became such a large number and mighty force that the Egyptians became afraid of their growing numbers and no longer remembered their close relationship of the past and chose instead to make them all slaves.

It happened just as God had told Abraham it would happen. But after years of slavery it finally came to an end approximately 1013 years after the flood or a total of 2669 years after Adam and Eve. This is an example of God's patience as He waited over 2000 years to reestablish what Adam and Eve had broken and to show a group of people how He wanted to protect them, bless them and have a relationship with them. God's plan was to deliver them from the oppression of Egypt once again with one man. When the Israelites cried out for help, He stepped in and raised up a man to rescue them. His name was Moses.

Moses was an Israelite who was raised as an Egyptian even though he was a Hebrew. Just like the story of Joseph, God can position His people to places of leadership and favor in amazing ways.

The Pharaoh of that day intended on killing the Hebrews, and yet God preserved Moses from death and actually put him under the Pharaoh's care. That was how Moses, even though he was born an Israelite, was raised as an Egyptian right in Pharaoh's house. In that act God orchestrated a rescue for the Israelites from the Egyptian slavery that would bring them into a land of promise.

Moses endured many things before he became that someone God could use. In fact, it involved hiding in the desert for about forty years as Moses gained insight into who God was and who he was. But when he emerged, he was ready to walk in the destiny for his life.

God, through Moses, gave Pharaoh the opportunity to *let* the Israelites go free. (Remember, there is always a choice.) But Pharaoh refused. He didn't want to give up such an army of free labor. And so when Pharaoh refused, God sent plagues upon the Egyptians and their land. This amazing story can be found in Exodus, chapters 7 through 11.

It took all ten supernatural signs for Pharaoh to finally release the slaves. It was a mighty display of supernatural power. That's what it took, not only for Pharaoh to recognize God's power, but for the Israelites to recognize Him as well. God reminded them of who He was, rescuing them out of a seemingly impossible situation.

> *"Then the Lord said to him, 'Know for certain that for four hundred years your descendants will be strangers in a country not their own and that they will be enslaved and mistreated there. But I will punish the nation they serve as slaves, and afterward they will come out with great possessions.'"*[59]

When Pharaoh was finally willing to release the Israelites from slavery, the Egyptian people *wanted* them to go. And just as the scripture above and below states, the Israelites came away not as slaves, but with great wealth.

"The Israelites did as Moses instructed and asked the Egyptians for articles of silver and gold and for clothing."[60]

As the Israelites left Egypt, God not only worked things out so His word was fulfilled and the people of Israel were set free, but His blessing came to His people as they left Egypt with great wealth. They left with the payment that had been due them from the years of slavery.

In my personal life God performed many miracles to rescue me from my own "Egypt" and to bring me to the freedom of His Kingdom. One aspect of this freedom is to have fulfilled the desire in my heart of owning my own business.

What I do every day to earn a living and support myself and my family is very important in my life. I believe God instilled this in us. If you recall, God put Adam in the Garden and gave him a job. He was to work and take care of the Garden. My father was an excellent car and truck mechanic, and in addition to his job working for the government, which provided just barely enough to make ends meet, he repaired cars in the evening and on the weekend. Dad was a hard worker and instilled the value of hard work in me.

When I was able to resign from working for someone else in order to start my own company, it was like leaving a place of "slavery." Not that my job was bad, but it was very restrictive and did not allow me to fully pursue what God had put in my heart to fulfill. The day I resigned, it was like walking out of "Egypt," and I was making my way into my "Promised Land." It is something that God wants to do for all of us. What is the Promised Land that God has for you?

"When Pharaoh let the people go, God did not lead them on the road through the Philistine country, though that was shorter. For God

MAPPING THE ROAD TO YOUR DESTINY

said, 'If they face war, they might change their minds and return to Egypt.'[61]

God led the people around by the desert road toward the Red Sea. God knew their weaknesses and the potential decisions they could make that would keep them from blessings. This illustrates how God made us with free will to make decisions. And so to protect them, He took them on a longer road to ensure they could get to their destiny. They were too far now to return to Egypt which was a place of slavery, but which was familiar.

How many times do I return to the familiar things in my life, even when they aren't the best thing for me? Pressing ahead into uncharted areas is always hard. Yet, even though God had proven He desired to bless the Israelites, they made many wrong choices. They complained. They disobeyed. Even as He provided for them in the wilderness, they made their own road so much harder as they refused to learn and understand the blessing that was just before them.

That same thing could happen in our lives still today. God has a destiny of purpose and blessing for each of us. And yet, He allows us the choice on what path we take. He will try to lead us on the path that will help us get there, but how often do we make that journey harder than it should be when we choose our own way and make our own decisions? And then we blame God when something goes wrong.

Over the years, especially as I was working to build my business, Lavonne and I learned that while there were certainly times His way didn't seem to make sense, I had learned enough about trusting Him to simply obey. I didn't have to, but I chose to, and I'm so glad that I did. I especially had to learn to trust Him in regard to finances. Initially when I started my business, I didn't have nearly enough money to get started. In my mind it would have made sense to keep everything that came in during that season so that hopefully we could pull together enough to launch out. But, He had taught us early in our marriage the importance of helping the poor and needy by giving of our income—even when it didn't look like it made any sense. And that's just it. God's ways *don't* always make sense. That is where relationship and trust come into the picture. Are we willing to choose that relationship and trust when we don't understand and when it doesn't make sense? Because that is the true foundation of relationship—and remember, that is what this is all about.

> *"And when the Israelites saw the mighty hand of the Lord displayed against the Egyptians, the people feared the Lord and put their trust in him and in Moses his servant."*[62]

Finally, after God rescued the Israelites from Egypt, it looks like trust and relationship between God and the Israelites were beginning to develop. It had already been around 1013 years since the flood where mankind had embraced evil of every sort, violence and corruption. It had been 621 years since the cities of Sodom and Gomorrah were destroyed for the evil and corruption within those cities. And yet God didn't give up on finding people who were willing to abandon their corruption and move forward to trust Him as the Creator of Heaven and Earth who loved them.

RULES AND REGULATIONS

At this point, God knows by experience that mankind left to their own with no guidance is not good and only produces wickedness, violence and corruption just as what happened during the first 1500 years of mankind.

Now God tries the opposite approach. He sets up specific rules and commands so the Israelites will know exactly what to do to live a prosperous life, pleasing to God. In turn God hopes to bring the rest of the people back to Him. But they had to choose it.

> *"The Lord issued a ruling and instruction for them and put them to the test. He said, 'If you listen carefully to the Lord your God and do what is right in his eyes, if you pay attention to his commands and keep all his decrees, I will not bring on you any of the diseases I brought on the Egyptians, for I am the Lord, who heals you.'"*[56]

God's plan and purpose is for us to listen to His voice, turn towards Him and do what He says, because that is what He knows is best for our end result. However, it is our decision to obey. And we will pay the price and reap the consequences for the decisions we make. There are blessings for listening to His voice and consequences for disobedience when we do not listen to His voice and simply choose to do things our own way.

Yet, it seems that mankind is incapable of listening to Him and following His instruction; and it is becoming obvious that even to receive the blessing, they are unable to make the choice to follow Him.

Remember the promise to Abraham to bless his descendants? This was a promise God repeated over and over. And because of that promise, He showed up over and over to help the Israelites and rescue them, even when they made poor decisions.

> *"Then Moses went up to God, and the Lord called to him from the mountain and said, 'This is what you are to say to the descendants of Jacob and what you are to tell the people of Israel: You yourselves have seen what I did to Egypt, and how I carried you on eagles' wings and brought you to myself. Now if you obey me fully and keep my covenant, then out of all nations you will be my treasured possession. Although the whole earth is mine, you will be for me a kingdom of priests and a holy nation. These are the words you are to speak to the Israelites.'"*[57]

Moses was a good leader with a heart for God. He spoke those words to the people and they responded, *"We will do everything the Lord has said."*[58]

So it looked like all was finally good. Abraham's descendants seem eager to follow God's ways. God wants to be their King, and they finally seem ready to do everything He says. It looks like they can finally see that God wants to help them and protect them as a father does his children. What an opportunity to have the Creator of the Universe offer to guide, direct and protect them and to establish His Kingdom through them! (A promise that is still in effect for us today.)

A ROCKY RELATIONSHIP

The Israelites knew how powerful God was when He rescued them from the oppression of the Egyptians. Wouldn't that be enough to encourage them to follow what He had outlined as the best path for them? But unfortunately, it wasn't.

The journey from Egypt to the Promised Land shouldn't have taken more than a week to a month with that size group estimated at a million people or more. Instead, the Israelites wandered in the desert for forty long years as they once again made their own choices and their own way.

During the years in the desert, God gave Moses some detailed commands on how to live at peace with Him and with each other. It was what is known today as the "Ten Commandments." The primary command from this set of instructions is the first and second. It seems to me as I read it that God simply wants them to worship Him alone and not other gods. If I think about it and put myself in His shoes, I would probably do the same thing. For example, when it comes to raising my children, I set in place a list of rules and commands and ask them to honor me by obedience to what I ask.

"Do not make any gods to be alongside me; do not make for yourselves gods of silver or gods of gold."[59]

Once again the Israelites were about to embark on an emotional roller coaster of their own making. They would obey and then disobey what God instructed. It caused great hardship for them, and for the next several hundred years God remained faithful to the relationship, even though they did not. He put up with their mistakes, sinful actions and disobedience.

When Moses came down the mountain from spending time with God, He had what we call "The Ten Commandments." Ten simple rules or guidelines on God's expectations for relationship, and yet they are given a choice whether to follow them or not. Isn't it interesting that it is these same Ten Commandments that are still controversial in our world today?

And yet when we look at them, why is it that we are so opposed to following them? Guidelines such as:

- Thou shalt not murder.

- Thou shalt not steal.

- Thou shalt not lie.

- Thou shalt not commit adultery.

- Honor your father and mother.

These are simply rules for success in life, aren't they? Perhaps it is that we don't like the fact that it is a "rule" or that someone else is telling us what to do. Or is it one of the other commandments which says,

- You shall have no other gods before Me.[60]

God wanted them to worship Him alone. This is very important to God. He recognized people's propensity to worship other things. But it is important to recognize that He provided these rules for them for success in life.

> *"The Lord said to Moses, 'Speak to the Israelites and say to them: "I am the Lord your God. You must not do as they do in Egypt, where you used to live, and you must not do as they do in the land of Canaan, where I am bringing you. Do not follow their practices. You must obey my laws and be careful to follow my decrees. I am the Lord your God. Keep my decrees and laws, for the person who obeys them will live by them. I am the Lord.."'"[61]*

Obviously, the way people lived around the Israelites is not pleasing to God, since He told them not to follow the practices of the Egyptians and the people living in Canaan where God was taking them.

What was it that these people from Egypt and Canaan were doing that God did not like? I can learn about what those practices are by examining the commands God told the Israelites to do and not to do.

202

For example, one area that I consider important in the world we live in today is sexual behavior. His commands in this area are very specific, clear and instructive. In some ways, as I read through those lists, it doesn't seem that people should even need to receive this type of instruction, but even today as I see the moral decline of society, it is obvious there was and is a need for these specific rules and the wisdom in providing them.

All of chapter 18 in the book of Leviticus is dedicated to provide for the Israelites specific rules of sexual behavior. God, through Moses, tells each Israelite not to have sexual relations with their mother, stepmother, sister, daughter, granddaughter, stepsister, aunt, daughter-in-law, sister-in-law, a woman and her daughter, a wife's sister while the wife is living, during her monthly period and their neighbor's wife.

God also instructed men not to have sexual relations with other men because that is detestable. He also instructed both men and women not to have sexual relations with an animal because that was a perversion. I consider it important to mention this because as it says in the New Covenant, *"Flee from sexual immorality. All other sins a person commits are outside the body, but whoever sins sexually, sins against their own body. Do you not know that your bodies are temples of the Holy Spirit, who is in you, whom you have received from God? You are not your own; you were bought at a price. Therefore, honor God with your bodies."*[62]

Today, I can't help but ask myself if God has changed His mind, and now He doesn't mind if we do any of these things He told the Israelites not to do. God was pretty clear and insisted several times on not doing any of these things.

"'Do not defile yourselves in any of these ways, because this is how the nations that I am going to drive out before you became defiled. Even the land was defiled; so I punished it for its sin, and the land vomited out its inhabitants. But you must keep my decrees and my laws. The native-born and the foreigners residing among you must not do any of these detestable things, for all these things were done by the people who

lived in the land before you, and the land became defiled. And if you defile the land, it will vomit you out as it vomited out the nations that were before you.

"Everyone who does any of these detestable things—such persons must be cut off from their people. Keep my requirements and do not follow any of the detestable customs that were practiced before you came and do not defile yourselves with them. I am the Lord your God."[63]

From these instructions, it is obvious that both the people of Egypt and those who were residing in the Promised Land were practicing this evil behavior. Because of that, God was willing to remove them and then give the land to the Israelites if they would live in a holy relationship with Him.

God had walked the Israelites out of slavery and now into the Promised Land. He wanted to make sure they understood that they were a special group of people whom He desired to bless and protect. We see this when He spoke to Moses: *"This is what you are to say to the descendants of Jacob and what you are to tell the people of Israel: 'You yourselves have seen what I did to Egypt, and how I carried you on eagles' wings and brought you to myself. Now if you obey me fully and keep my covenant, then out of all nations you will be my treasured possession. Although the whole earth is mine, you will be for me a kingdom of priests and a holy nation."[64]*

Although it seemed to work for a while and although the people expressed that they had a heart to follow after God and His command-ments, the reality was they often did their own thing. They were obedient at one juncture, but at the very next opportunity they began to complain, argue, kill and follow after other gods.

Although God chose the Israelites, it was not a guarantee that they could do whatever they wanted with no consequences. That is because God is a holy God and sets the standard. He is very clear with them what He desires and commands in order for them to live in peace and to be prosperous. It would be hard for them to say they didn't understand how to behave holy, for they were given the commandments and continued instruction for personal behaviors that would bring blessings to them. Other commands include, for example:

- Do not lie.

- Do not steal.

- Do not hold back the wages of a hired man overnight.

- Do not practice divination or sorcery.

- Do not prevent justice.

Check these out:

- Be nice to the poor.

- Do not cheat people.

- Do not be unjust.

- Respect the elderly.

- Do not mistreat the alien living among you.

- Be honest.

I would say that if all of us follow these commands individually and collectively, a lot of the world problems we face today would just disappear!

God was preparing them as they walked through the desert from Egypt to the Promised Land, how to take the land and live in the land successfully. But because of their grumbling and disobedience, the journey was prolonged to forty years. When they finally did emerge from the wilderness to receive the land promised, it then took them another forty-five years to fight and drive out the inhabitants of the land.

Why didn't God just remove the people that inhabited the Promise Land all at once? I believe it is because He knows that it is in the challenges of life where we have to press in and overcome that we gain strength, insight and perspective.

During that time God often fought for them. He performed many miraculous signs to show them that with God they could have victory over their enemies.

The Israelites also learned that as long as they would walk in obedience to the rules and commands God provided and give Him proper credit, they knew He would continue to bless them.

Moses also made it clear that the Israelites were being given the Promised Land, not so much because of their pure lives, but because God was removing the wicked people currently occupying the land. They simply had to listen to His voice and enter into relationship with Him in order to take the land and receive the blessing.

Finally, they were instructed on the importance of passing these instructions on to their children and their children's children in order that they also would prosper in the land.

> *"So the Lord gave Israel all the land he had sworn to give their ancestors, and they took possession of it and settled there. The Lord gave them rest on every side, just as he had sworn to their ancestors. Not one of their enemies withstood them; the Lord gave all their enemies into their hands. Not one of all the Lord's good promises to Israel failed; every one was fulfilled."*[65]

After Moses' death and under Joshua's leadership, the Israelites enjoyed twenty-five years of peace. But then things began going downhill—and fast.

Chapter 8

THE ENDLESS CYCLE OF GOOD AND EVIL

Unbelievably, following the death of Joshua, the next generation of Israelites forgot what God had done for them. *"After that whole generation had been gathered to their ancestors, another generation grew up who knew neither the Lord nor what he had done for Israel. Then the Israelites did evil in the eyes of the Lord and served the Baals. They forsook the Lord, the God of their ancestors, who had brought them out of Egypt. They followed and worshiped various gods of the peoples around them. They aroused the Lord's anger because they forsook him and served Baal and the Ashtoreths. In his anger against Israel the Lord gave them into the hands of raiders who plundered them. He sold them into the hands of their enemies all around, whom they were no longer able to resist. Whenever Israel went out to fight, the hand of the Lord was against them to defeat them, just as he had sworn to them. They were in great distress."* [66]

How did the next generation grow up neither knowing the Lord nor what He had done for their parents? It's hard to imagine with all the

207

mighty miracles their ancestors experienced with their release from the evil Pharaoh from Egypt, the parting of the Red Sea, the provision of food in the wilderness and how they were able to inhabit the Promised Land, that now they had already forsaken God.

What happened?

Did the next generation just choose to ignore God, or did their parents forget to pass on those stories as instructed? I don't know the answer, but what is clear is that they pushed God away and started to worship idols which caused them to live in great distress losing against all their enemies.

Can you imagine how that must grieve God? He wanted to bless them. He wanted relationship with them. Over and over He proved Himself faithful to them and they proved themselves faithless to Him. They walked away from Him to pursue and worship other gods even as He held His hand out to them.

God's desire was to bless them and to use them as an example to bring other people to Himself rather than the other way around as is happening here. But God does not seem to give up on them yet. He still wants to try again to make this relationship work.

"Then the Lord raised up judges, who saved them out of the hands of these raiders." [67]

God provided them with judges/leaders in the land to provide wisdom, instruction and help. Unfortunately, that did not work out either because the people refused to listen to their judges.[68] And yet the Lord *still* had compassion for them.

"Whenever the Lord raised up a judge for them, he was with the judge and saved them out of the hands of their enemies as long as the judge lived; for the Lord relented because of their groaning under those who oppressed and afflicted them." [69] This shows clearly the heart of the Father toward His children.

A quick overview that follows reveals a clearer picture. When they chose to turn to God, they experienced blessing. When they chose to disobey God, they experienced a curse. After the Israelites entered the Promised Land:

- They lived in peace for twenty-five years under the leadership of Joshua as they obeyed God.

- They chose to disobey God and so they lived eight years of misery as slaves under the rule of King Aram.

- This was followed by repentance and a forty-year stretch of peace under the leadership of Othniel.

- As they disobeyed God again, they lived eighteen years of misery under the rule of the king of Moab.

- Once again they repented and lived for eighty years in peace under Ehud.

- Followed by twenty years of grief and slavery under the king of Canaan.

- They cried out to God and He raised up Deborah to be their judge/leader, and they experienced peace for forty years.

- Followed by seven years of miserable slavery under the Midianites.

- They experienced forty years of peace under the rule of Gideon as once again they turned back to God.

- Followed three years of hardship under Abimelech as they chose to follow their own ways and do evil.

- Once again they repented and God raised up Jair of Gilead who led them, and they had peace for twenty-two years.

- Followed by eighteen years of misery under the oppressive rule of the Philistines and Ammonites when they chose to once again walk away from God.

During this repetitive cycle they forsook God six times, but each time to their own hurt. They experienced 245 years of peace when they chose to follow and listen to Him compared to seventy-four years of misery and slavery when they chose their own way. It seems hard to imagine that they couldn't see the connection between the years of a peaceful and prosperous life when they were obedient to God, to the years of oppression they experienced at the hand of other nations and the miserable life that followed when they chose to walk away from God.

Do you see the connection? I believe it still exists in the world today. The moment I make the decision to push God away from my life and walk my own path, I remove myself from His blessing and I am on my own.

This cycle continues as once again the people cry out to God. He hears them and with a heart of compassion still loves them and so provides them with other judges who will help them and impart wisdom to them on how to live a successful life; but after another 150 years, the same pattern continued. It was clear that the people simply weren't willing to allow God to be their King. And in fact, they demanded an earthly king to rule over them. This truly grieved God's heart. For in making that demand, what they were truly saying was, "God, You are not our King. We want a king here to rule over us." And so, they demanded of the prophet Samuel, whom God had given them as a spiritual leader, to give them a king.

> *"So all the elders of Israel gathered together and came to Samuel at Ramah. They said to him, 'You are old, and your sons do not follow your ways; now appoint a king to lead us, such as all the other nations have.'"[70]*

God knew this was not a wise request and would not be a good thing for them. As a Father, it had to have hurt His heart. And yet, He gave them the choice of their own will and said to Samuel:

"Listen to all that the people are saying to you; it is not you they have rejected, but they have rejected me as their king. As they have done from the day I brought them up out of Egypt until this day, forsaking me and serving other gods, so they are doing to you. Now listen to them; but warn them solemnly and let them know what the king who will reign over them will claim as his rights."[71]

Before they are given their wish, God warns them through Samuel about the consequences of their choice for a human king instead of letting God be their King. They are told how the king will oppress them with taxes. He will make them slaves and take their children. He will take the best of their produce and catapult them into war. But despite the warnings they receive, they *still* choose that path. And it turned out exactly as God had warned them as kings began to rule the land and the people.

From that point on the Israelites were led by kings rather than judges. The first was Saul who reigned over them for forty-two years. That was followed by King David who reigned for forty years followed by his son, Solomon.

As God had predicted, the kings taxed the people. They catapulted them into war. King Saul turned out to not be a good king and so God gave the kingdom to a shepherd named David. It is said that David had a "heart after God." But David also sinned and experienced numerous challenges and yet He sought to restore the people back to God. Finally, it was through the reign of his son, Solomon, that we see God's intent again to live with His people. David had wanted to build a temple for God to honor Him and worship Him, but it was his son, King Solomon, who actually undertook the construction of the magnificent building project.

God continues to repeat the same message He has been repeating for several hundred years. This time when Solomon was building the temple, God told him, *"As for this temple you are building, if you follow my decrees, observe my laws and keep all my commands and obey them, I will fulfill through*

211

you the promise I gave to David your father. And I will live among the Israelites and will not abandon my people Israel."[72]

God's plan was and still is to live among His people. Once again His heart and purpose were clear. He longed to be in the midst of the people He created. Solomon built what was recorded as one of the most luxurious and magnificent structures ever created overlaid with gold, jewels and expensive tapestries. Solomon was known for being very wise and rich.

"King Solomon was greater in riches and wisdom than all the other kings of the earth."[73]

"From all nations people came to listen to Solomon's wisdom, sent by all the kings of the world, who had heard of his wisdom"[74]

All this wisdom was given to him by God. "God gave Solomon wisdom and very great insight, and a breadth of understanding as measureless as the sand on the seashore."[75]

However, in spite of all this wisdom, Solomon had a weak point in his life which ended up bringing destruction to all he had done.

"King Solomon, however, loved many foreign women...."[76]

The problem with that was that these women were from nations which the Lord had clearly instructed the Israelites, *"You must not intermarry with them."[77]* And He tells him specifically why: *"Because they will surely turn your hearts after their gods."[78]*

Solomon chose to forget what God had said and *"held fast to them in love."[79]* And it wasn't just one or two or three foreign wives. Solomon had 700 foreign wives, and in addition to that he had 300 concubines! But just as God had said, *"As Solomon grew old, his wives turned his heart after other gods, and his heart was not fully devoted to the Lord his God, as the heart of David his father had been."[80]*

In the end he is remembered as doing evil in the eyes of the Lord contrary to his father who had been a godly king. This angered God, and as a result, He split the kingdom of Israel in two just as Solomon's heart was divided between God and foreign gods. Israel became the kingdom of Israel and the kingdom of Judah.

The relationship of the Israelites with God went from bad to worse, so that for the next 243 years, of nineteen kings who reigned over the kingdom of Israel, only one, King Jehu, honored God for twenty-eight years. The numbers really don't look good. Ninety-five percent of the kings did evil, and only 12 percent of this time did they honor God.

I can see why God warned them not to get a king. He wanted to be their King, but they refused. And at the end of the 243 years, as they continued to ignore God and behave wickedly, God allowed the king of Assyria to conquer their kingdom and deport them to Assyria as slaves.

"All this took place because the Israelites had sinned against the Lord their God, who had brought them up out of Egypt from under the power of Pharaoh king of Egypt. They worshiped other gods and followed the practices of the nations the Lord had driven out before them, as well as the practices that the kings of Israel had introduced. The Israelites secretly did things against the Lord their God that were not right. From watchtower to fortified city they built themselves high places in all their towns. They set up sacred stones and Asherah poles on every high hill and under every spreading tree. At every high place they burned incense, as the nations whom the Lord had driven out before them had done. They did wicked things that aroused the Lord's anger. They worshiped idols, though the Lord had said, 'You shall not do this.' The Lord warned Israel and Judah through all his prophets and seers: 'Turn from your evil ways. Observe my commands and decrees, in accordance with the entire Law that I commanded your ancestors to obey and that I delivered to you through my servants the prophets.'

"But they would not listen and were as stiff-necked as their ancestors, who did not trust in the Lord their God. They rejected his decrees and the covenant he had made with their ancestors and the statutes he

had warned them to keep. They followed worthless idols and themselves became worthless. They imitated the nations around them although the Lord had ordered them, 'Do not do as they do.'

"They forsook all the commands of the Lord their God and made for themselves two idols cast in the shape of calves, and an Asherah pole. They bowed down to all the starry hosts, and they worshiped Baal. They sacrificed their sons and daughters in the fire. They practiced divination and sought omens and sold themselves to do evil in the eyes of the Lord, arousing his anger.

"So the Lord was very angry with Israel and removed them from his presence. Only the tribe of Judah was left, and even Judah did not keep the commands of the Lord their God. They followed the practices Israel had introduced. Therefore the Lord rejected all the people of Israel; he afflicted them and gave them into the hands of plunderers, until he thrust them from his presence."[81]

The Israelites had completely rejected God as each different group created their own gods and erected shrines and offered sacrifices to them… often their own children. [82]

This was a barbaric practice that accentuates the evil that had overtaken their hearts. God was very specific that He abhorred this practice. *"Do not give any of your children to be sacrificed to Molek, for you must not profane the name of your God. I am the Lord."*[83] Who would sacrifice their own child to a man-made god? If they were so intent on offering a sacrifice, why not offer themselves? But I can see this in history from then to the present that as a society moves away from God, it becomes more influenced by the culture around it. For example, is abortion any different as we offer up the sacrifice of our children to the "god" of our own convenience and "rights"? Why are the children the ones who pay the price for the deeds of the adults? It is a cycle that continues from the past.

Once the Israelites from the kingdom of Israel were taken away to Assyria, the kingdom of Judah remained in Israel for another 114 years. Let's look at how they fared.

In the 357 years that followed after King Solomon's reign, they had twenty kings. Eight of them "did good in the eyes of the Lord," and twelve did evil. The eight that did good did it for 227 years. But the numbers didn't look good either. Sixty percent of the kings were evil and 36 percent of the time they spent doing evil. If we compare this to a marriage, it would be like one spouse cheating on the other a third of the time. That's certainly not a good recipe if the relationship is to last.

Eventually God grew weary of this roller coaster and Judah's inconsistent heart for Him and used Nebuchadnezzar, the king of Babylon, to conquer them and then he took them into exile into Babylon. Once again, by their own acts and choices, the Israelites were slaves. This didn't happen overnight. Prior to it, God had sent them prophet after prophet, warning them that if their actions didn't change that their enemies would eventually defeat them and make them slaves. And eventually it came to pass.

As I look at this history, it is important to remember that God always remained faithful to the people of Israel. He also remained faithful to Himself for He cannot do otherwise. He is a holy God and a just God and always acts and responds from those two places.

It is at His core that He is just and He requires an impartial system of justice—one that is fair and honest and calls evil what is evil and good what is good. He desires justice for everyone. When we belong to His Kingdom, we can trust that He will bring justice where there is injustice for us personally. God is a judge who sees everyone's heart and motives. If you have experienced injustice, you can run to Him, for *"will not God bring about justice for his chosen ones, who cry out to him day and night? Will he keep putting them off? I tell you, he will see that they get justice, and quickly."*[84]

Most of us have at one time or another experienced injustice, and it is a painful experience. Before I started my own business, I personally felt

I did not get justice or that I was treated fairly. I made the decision to let God be the judge and to pay me back instead of pursuing a justice system created by man. I can tell you that God rewarded me far more than I could imagine. I learned firsthand that He is indeed a God of justice. And if I let Him be the judge, I know I will receive justice.

When I am willing to trust God with my life and trust Him to bring about justice, I then empower Him to operate on my behalf. Remember, He *desires* to bless us and be in relationship with us. I believe He is just waiting for us to call on Him.

There are numerous cases where we see this in the Bible where an act of obedience and trust in God in unjust situations became a catalyst for a mighty miracle. One such case is the story of three Israelites named Shadrach, Meshach and Abednego.

This took place when the Israelites from the kingdom of Judah had been carried into exile into Babylon. These three men were part of the team of wise men who had been put into King Nebuchadnezzar's service. Yet, although they were required to serve before this earthly king, these three men had hearts that were truly serving God.

King Nebuchadnezzar built a golden image of himself that was ninety feet tall. He then ordered all the people in the land to bow before it. Only Shadrach, Meshach and Abednego respectfully refused. They had served the king well, but they would not dishonor God, the King of kings. King Nebuchadnezzar was furious. He gave them a second chance with the threat that they would be thrown in the fiery furnace if they refused to bow.

The three said without hesitation, *"King Nebuchadnezzar, we do not need to defend ourselves before you in this matter. If we are thrown into the blazing furnace, the God we serve is able to deliver us from it, and he will deliver us from Your Majesty's hand. But even if he does not, we want you to know, Your Majesty, that we will not serve your gods or worship the image of gold you have set up."*[85]

What faith and strength these men had in the face of death as they held to their belief in the living God. Nebuchadnezzar was so enraged by their act that he had the furnace stoked seven times hotter than normal. In fact, it was so hot that it instantly killed the soldiers who pushed Shadrach, Meshach and Abednego into the furnace. And yet, it didn't kill those three. It says that the king looked into the fire and saw not just those three walking around in the fire, but a fourth "man" as well.

> *"Then King Nebuchadnezzar leaped to his feet in amazement and asked his advisers, 'Weren't there three men that we tied up and threw into the fire?'*

> *"They replied, 'Certainly, Your Majesty.'*

> *"He said, 'Look! I see four men walking around in the fire, unbound and unharmed, and the fourth looks like a son of the gods.'"*[86]

At this the king realized what had happened and changed his attitude completely. He asked them to come out of the furnace. Then the king said, *"Praise be to the God of Shadrach, Meshach and Abednego, who has sent his angel and rescued his servants!"*[87] Not only did this earthly king end up praising and worshipping the real God, but he also commanded the people of his kingdom to respect God. He ruled, *"Therefore I decree that the people of any nation or language who say anything against the God of Shadrach, Meshach and Abednego be cut into pieces and their houses be turned into piles of rubble, for no other god can save in this way."*[88]

This king had a complete transformation when he saw firsthand the power of God.

Their faith became the catalyst to allow God to perform a miracle on their behalf. For you see, God is waiting on us to invite Him into our lives and for relationship. He doesn't mind being put in these positions. In fact, He rather likes it when we treat Him as the God He is. It not only allows Him to show us His love and protection for us, but it allows those who do not believe a chance to see Him for who He is.

Today it is not popular to refuse to bow down to the idols of our modern culture such as sexual immorality, political correctness and corruption. If I refuse to bow down to the idols of our current culture, I may not face a physical fiery furnace, but I may face isolation, ridicule, abuse or harrassment. But when I make my decisions based on what is pleasing to God, and honor Him, I am convinced He will honor me and protect me.

Their response to the king as they faced the threat of death is a powerful display of those who have given their all to Him.

> *"King Nebuchadnezzar, we do not need to defend ourselves before you in this matter. If we are thrown into the blazing furnace, the God we serve is able to deliver us from it, and he will deliver us from Your Majesty's hand. But even if he does not, we want you to know, Your Majesty, that we will not serve your gods or worship the image of gold you have set up."*[89]

The fact that they were willing to die, even if God did not do what they told the king God could do, demonstrates a very deep and solid commitment to God. This is what I call being free, complete freedom, when I am willing to lose it all for God.

I can't help but question myself, if I were in similar circumstances, would I be willing to take a stand for my beliefs even if it meant possible death? That is definitely a tough question and I don't know the answer, but I hope these three guys will be an inspiration to me.

When we begin to understand that the Bible is more than a book of history, but actually a life-shaping and life-changing book of instruction for our lives that will lead us into a life of miracles and blessings, that is when it transforms us.

So, what does transformation look like?

Chapter 9

GOD'S NEW PLAN

The word "transformation" means: to change in composition or structure, to change the outward form or appearance of or to change in character or condition.[90]

What about your life? Is it time for a transformation? Does God have a specific plan for you? I can assure you that He does. It's just a matter of allowing Him to guide you to it, and it's not as complicated as you might think.

When I understood that God was real and that the Bible was a book not only of the past, but the present and the future, that is when my transformation really took hold. As I launched my own business with no money and little help, I look back and see His hand guiding each and every step of the way. I marvel at how every job I had, the relationships I made along the way, and how my journey intersected with others, was all part of a preparation process to enable me to fulfill the dream He had planted in my heart for my own business. I didn't know how I would get there, but the more I gave Him of myself, the more He continued to direct my steps. I recognize now that so much was based on trusting Him and the process much like Shadrach, Meschach and Abednego had trusted Him. It can be a scary place. But it is a place where He shows up and where He wants to show up for you.

I hear that a smart person learns from his or her mistakes, but a wise person learns from the mistakes of others. As I continue to look over the ups and downs of the Israelites' relationship with God and their lack of truly turning to Him, I can learn a lot from their mistakes. They didn't put their complete trust in Him. They allowed other ungodly cultures to influence them instead of them influencing the other cultures. They continued to do their own thing time and again, and they paid a huge price each time. It doesn't make sense.

But God is still God. He is still the same yesterday, today and tomorrow. He still wants to be treated as God and live among His creation. At the point when the Israelites were taken into exile to other kingdoms, it had been approximately 1582 years since God had hoped to establish His Kingdom here on earth through them. And it had been 3606 years since He had tried through Adam and Eve. Instead of growing closer to God over the centuries, mankind was actually growing further and further apart. Yet, God's promise to them then is still His promise to us today in which He desires relationship with us and to bless us.

As I said before during the first 1500 years, mankind lived with no rules or commands from God, and the results were not good. Evil was in control of mankind.

> *"The Lord saw how great the wickedness of the human race had become on the earth, and that every inclination of the thoughts of the human heart was only evil all the time. The Lord regretted that he had made human beings on the earth, and his heart was deeply troubled."*[91]

After this fiasco, God decided to go completely the other way and set up very specific rules for the group of people He wants to use to show the world how to live God's way. That's why He chose Abraham and made the Israelites His people. After God rescued Abraham's descendants from

400 years of oppression, He gave them specific rules to live by. They were supposed to show the world God's way. Yet, He tried and tried for another 1500 years, but it did not work then either, for the people kept turning away from God's rules and commands to follow ungodly practices of other people. It looked like evil won again. Once again He realized that man wasn't capable of not sinning; his inclination was always to move away from God.

Given these results, God decided to establish a new plan. This time He was going to defeat evil Himself by coming to earth as a human being and provide us a way back into relationship with Him. This time it would not be by following rules or commands, but by just believing in Him. This is known as the New Covenant.

During some of the reigns of the last kings of both Judah and Israel, God started to speak through prophets of this new plan. We can see this, for example, in the books of Isaiah, Jeremiah and Ezekiel. They introduced the plan that was to come. It was something completely new which would be called the New Covenant or New Testament which was to set people free from darkness and oppression.

> *"I, the LORD, have called you in righteousness; I will take hold of your hand. I will keep you and will make you to be a covenant for the people and a light for the Gentiles, to open eyes that are blind, to free captives from prison and to release from the dungeon those who sit in darkness.*
>
> *"I am the LORD; that is my name! I will not yield my glory to another or my praise to idols. See, the former things have taken place, and new things I declare; before they spring into being I announce them to you."*[92]

Here are some additional prophecies He made. In each one take note of the word "covenant."

> *"'The days are coming,' declares the Lord, 'when I will make a new covenant with the people of Israel and with the people of Judah. It will not be like the covenant I made with their ancestors when I took them by the hand to lead them out of Egypt, because they broke my covenant, though I was a husband to them,' declares the Lord. 'This is the covenant I will make with the people of Israel after that time,' declares the Lord. 'I will put my law in their minds and write it on their hearts. I will be their God, and they will be my people. No longer will they teach their neighbor, or say to one another, "Know the Lord," because they will all know me, from the least of them to the greatest,' declares the Lord. 'For I will forgive their wickedness and will remember their sins no more.'"93*

Here I see an amazing thing has happened, but to understand it I have to first understand the difference between a covenant and a contract. In a contract, if either party breaks the terms set within the agreement, then the contract itself is broken. However, that isn't true in a covenant. In a covenant, a violation by one party in the agreement doesn't matter or change the outcome as far as the other party's responsibility to continue to do what they agreed to do. What that means is even when I may fail in my relationship with God, it doesn't change how He responds to me because of His promise through His covenant to me.

This is an amazing thing that gives me hope. For with this New Covenant, no longer would it be dependent on mankind which had failed time and again. Now in order to set up this New Covenant with us, God would Himself come to earth and confront evil face-to-face as a man. He did this by sending His Son, Jesus Christ, to come to earth, born as a man to overcome evil and the power of sin which was continually separating us from a relationship with God. Why did it take that? Because if you remember in the Garden of Eden, God told Adam that if he disobeyed and ate from the fruit of the tree of knowledge of good and evil that he would die. Death and sin were set in motion at that point when Adam and Eve disobeyed. In order to cancel that sin, a death had to take place. Once that price was paid, evil would lose its grip on us. God was willing to pay the ultimate price when He sent His Son to die in our place to erase that debt. So God did it. Approximately 4000 years after Adam and Eve, He came to earth to start this New Covenant.

"In the beginning was the Word, and the Word was with God, and the Word was God. He was with God in the beginning... The Word became flesh and made his dwelling among us. We have seen his glory, the glory of the one and only Son, who came from the Father, full of grace and truth."[94]

This refers to Jesus when He was born on earth as a man. He was born in Bethlehem in the land of Israel.

Jesus lived on the earth thirty-three years. He spent the last three years of His life here teaching and demonstrating God's miraculous power. He showed us what the Kingdom of God looked like. He demonstrated God's love to us through His life.

"He came to that which was his own, but his own did not receive him. Yet to all who did receive him, to those who believed in his name, he gave the right to become children of God."[95]

When Jesus was here He taught that the Kingdom of God was different from the kingdom that had been established in the world. Now the Kingdom of God is inside everyone who believes in Him. His teachings go against what logic would say is reasonable. Teachings such as:

- Love your enemies and pray for those who persecute you.[96]

- If someone wants to sue you to take something from you, give him more than what he wants.[97]

- If someone asks you for your help, then do not turn him or her away.

- Do unto others as you would have them do to you.[98]

I don't have to meditate on those statements for too long to realize that a great majority of our current social and world problems would disappear if we would just be willing to do things God's way.

So why don't we follow these simple teachings? Why is it so hard? From the beginning of time this conflict has existed, and it started in the Garden of Eden when Adam and Eve chose to follow their own way and gave entrance to evil into the world.

Evil does not want these teachings to be embraced because evil thrives on violence, hate, selfishness, corruption and destruction. Evil has a good grip on this world, and it has infiltrated every area of society. Don't believe me? Just look around and consider the culture around you and in the world at large. We only have to look at what is playing on the television, movies, news, phones or what is being published in our books and even in our new governmental laws. Do these encourage you to live pure and cultivate a relationship with God, or do they mock those teachings? Do they encourage us to live for God or live for ourselves?

The answer to that is simple. Our present culture seeks to push us away from God, and many have been deceived and chosen to do just that. Evil hasn't changed much in the last 6000 years, has it?

Yet God has made a covenant with us. Remember that the agreement isn't broken even if one party breaks their side, so even when we are not faithful in a relationship with Him, He remains faithful to us. He still wants to have a relationship with the people He created and bring them into the blessings of His Kingdom. That is why He sent His Son, Jesus, to come to earth to establish this New Covenant that would provide a bridge to have relationship with Him once and for all for those who would choose it. He continues to have compassion on us and extend mercy to us.

When I study the life of Jesus, I see a Man who healed the sick, who had compassion on people, who reached out to those who were oppressed, who provided and fed multitudes of people and restored the lives of those who were hopeless. He taught the secret on how to live a life full of joy. That secret is still available to us today.

The secret is simply to choose Him. He said this with the simple statement, *"I am the way and the truth and the life. No one comes to the Father except through me."[99]*

At the time Jesus said these words it didn't go over well with some of the leaders of the people, so they made a plot and convinced the government authorities to kill Him. Even today those words don't go over very well with many people. Why? I believe it is because it puts them on a path to have to decide if they would choose Him or not.

The government authorities had Jesus beaten, abused and hung on a cross to die. His death was foretold by the prophets. *"But he was pierced for our transgressions, he was crushed for our iniquities; the punishment that brought us peace was on him, and by his wounds we are healed."[100]*

"When you were dead in your sins and in the uncircumcision of your flesh, God made you alive with Christ. He forgave us all our sins, having canceled the charge of our legal indebtedness, which stood against us and condemned us; he has taken it away, nailing it to the cross. And having disarmed the powers and authorities, he made a public spectacle of them, triumphing over them by the cross."[101]

It was because of God's willingness to die for us that opened the door for us to finally have that relationship that He desired with His creation from the beginning. It provided a way you and I could be healed in our hearts and our bodies. It is a promise made through a covenant that still stands true and available to us today.

So why do I share all of this? Simply to tell you that the moment you believe in Jesus Christ as the Son of God and confess with your mouth that He is Lord of your life, you are transformed into members of His Kingdom. When we become members of His Kingdom, we become righteous not of our own doing, but because of what He did. Also, we can approach

Him as sons and daughters and call Him God, King, Father and Friend. As the scripture says, we become descendants of Abraham and so we are heirs according to the promise of God.[102] All the promises and blessings that He outlined for Abraham and for the Israelites in the days long ago, He has given to us when we believe.

God is ready and desires to guide you into your own Promised Land of blessing. He has never changed. Just as He desired to take the Israelites out of slavery into a land of overwhelming blessing, so He desires to do that with each one of us. He desires to do that for you.

It may have looked like Jesus lost the day He was crucified, but in fact, He actually won. He beat evil that day, but evil is still trying to hide that truth and hide the existence of these promises available to us.

I believe that the most important thing that you need to know at this moment is that it doesn't matter what you have done in the past. You also don't have to "get everything right" before coming to God. It only takes a decision to come to Him and believe and your life will change.

> "Therefore, if anyone is in Christ, the new creation has come: The old has gone, the new is here! All this is from God, who reconciled us to himself through Christ and gave us the ministry of reconciliation: that God was reconciling the world to himself in Christ, not counting people's sins against them. And he has committed to us the message of reconciliation."[103]

What will this cost you?

Nothing.

I mean everything.

For this is His free gift to you to either receive it or reject it. You have nothing to lose except the heartache and emptiness that can be found in living the way of the kingdom of the world. But you have everything to gain. God doesn't want just part of you. He wants everything.

He is calling to you now and that is the tug in your heart, for He says:

"Here I am! I stand at the door and knock. If anyone hears my voice and opens the door, I will come in and eat with that person, and they with me."[104]

He is simply waiting for you. If you give Him a chance, He is ready to show Himself to you and demonstrate His love for you!

Many people wait until they are desperate, until there is no hope, until they have to reach up to touch bottom to give God a chance in their lives. That is not necessary. God wants to have a relationship with you now.

You can make that decision now by simply asking Him and praying this prayer or one straight from your heart:

Jesus, I believe You are the Son of God. I believe You died for me. I ask You to change me and forgive me of my past and to heal my heart. Please guide my life and the future You have for me. I choose You as You have chosen me.

I tell you, when you do that, you leave behind the kingdom of the world and enter into the Kingdom of God. You are now saved and have created a big party in heaven! Jesus said, *"In the same way, I tell you, there is rejoicing in the presence of the angels of God over one sinner who repents."*[105]

So what do you do now?

I suggest you begin to read the Bible from start to finish. It may not make complete sense at first like what happened to me, but I guarantee that as you continue reading and ask God to reveal the meaning to you, it will begin to click. He has given His promise and His blessings personally to you, and you can find them as you read the pages of the message He has for your life. But remember, this is not the end. There is a lot left.

What does the future hold for us? The last book of the Bible gives us a picture of how it is going to be. It reveals that it is going to be just as it was in the beginning.

"Then I saw 'a new heaven and a new earth,' for the first heaven and the first earth had passed away, and there was no longer any sea.

"I saw the Holy City, the new Jerusalem, coming down out of heaven from God, prepared as a bride beautifully dressed for her husband. And I heard a loud voice from the throne saying, 'Look! God's dwelling place is now among the people, and he will dwell with them. They will be his people, and God himself will be with them and be their God. He will wipe every tear from their eyes. There will be no more death' or mourning or crying or pain, for the old order of things has passed away.

"He who was seated on the throne said, 'I am making everything new!' Then he said, 'Write this down, for these words are trustworthy and true.'"[106]

There you have it again. God has always wanted to hang out with us, and that is how it is going to be forever with God living among His people and being their God. He offers you and me that opportunity to start now.

"He said to me: 'It is done. I am the Alpha and the Omega, the Beginning and the End. To the thirsty I will give water without cost from the spring of the water of life. Those who are victorious will inherit all this, and I will be their God and they will be my children. But the cowardly, the unbelieving, the vile, the murderers, the sexually immoral, those who practice magic arts, the idolaters and all liars— they will be consigned to the fiery lake of burning sulfur. This is the second death.'"[107]

What does the "second death" mean? I believe it means the eternal separation from God. But with the New Covenant provided through the sacrifice of Jesus, He provided a way of salvation for us to bypass this second death. Eventually we all will die a physical death, but His promise is that for all who will receive and believe in Him we will have eternal life spiritually bypassing the second death.

228

I do not know about you, but a fiery lake of burning sulfur does not sound very appealing to me. I don't think it is worth the risk to spend eternity over there. I don't have to and you don't have to either. He loves us so much that He made it really easy for you and me to be reconciled with Him and be part of His Kingdom.

God also knows that we are surrounded by evil and need help—a lot of help—on earth even after we are saved.

"But the Advocate, the Holy Spirit, whom the Father will send in my name, will teach you all things and will remind you of everything I have said to you."[108]

If you prayed that prayer of salvation, you now have eternal life with God; but not only that, while we live here on earth He has given us the Holy Spirit.

The Holy Spirit is given to us to help us in our lives here on earth. He will speak to us, guide us and help us through everything we face or encounter.

"So I say to you: Ask and it will be given to you; seek and you will find; knock and the door will be opened to you. For everyone who asks receives; the one who seeks finds; and to the one who knocks, the door will be opened. Which of you fathers, if your son asks for a fish, will give him a snake instead? Or if he asks for an egg, will give him a scorpion? If you then, though you are evil, know how to give good gifts to your children, how much more will your Father in heaven give the Holy Spirit to those who ask him!"[109]

The first time I read this scripture, I just did what it says. I stopped reading and I asked God to give me the Holy Spirit. I believe I received the Holy Spirit right then just because I did it in faith, taking God at His Word.

The Holy Spirit is your companion now, and He is available to help you. Although we have received Jesus into our heart and He knows us now, it doesn't mean life is without any challenges, but the Holy Spirit will be there to help us through each and every challenge. You will still face temptations, for evil still exists on this earth. There will still be the opportunity to worry about the future, to fear the unknown, to battle sickness and other storms of life, but you will never have to face them alone. Once you become a child of God, then it transports you back to the Garden of Eden in that you are in fellowship with God and nothing can separate you from Him.

> *"For I am convinced that neither death nor life, neither angels nor demons, neither the present nor the future, nor any powers, neither height nor depth, nor anything else in all creation, will be able to separate us from the love of God that is in Christ Jesus our Lord."*[110]

Does this all sound foolish to you? It does to many who have yet to believe in Him. But when we say we are willing to believe, then that is when clarity to this message can truly come.

> *"The person without the Spirit does not accept the things that come from the Spirit of God but considers them foolishness, and cannot understand them because they are discerned only through the Spirit."*[111]

I hope that this short summary of the Bible, if nothing else, helped you to understand how much God loves you and that He has a plan for you. He wants to spend time with you personally and hang out with you. You never have to try to make it on your own again, because He is there for you if you will just ask and give Him a chance in your life.

I can tell you that putting these thoughts in writing has helped me more than I imagined. It allowed me to have a greater overview of God's plan and His love which are available to us all.

So what is the next step? It is to hang out with Him. Get to know Him, and one way to do that is to get to know what He says in His Word—the Bible. In the back I have included some scriptures that helped me when I encountered various challenges in my life. I encourage you to read them and commit them to memory, for that will give you success on this journey.

I am still learning. I am a work in progress. Life is a journey, but now I can grab His hand and walk with the One who loves me the most and will guide me along a safe path so that I can fulfill my destiny.

Chapter 10

AVOIDING THE POTHOLES OF LIFE

Today, God still delivers people and supernaturally moves in their lives. I hope you can see that in my story of how God rescued me as a poor kid from the dirt roads of Costa Rica and empowered me to run a successful company. It is only because of His grace, goodness, wisdom, mercy and power that I have been able to see my dreams come true. Now I am living in my Promised Land.

Remember, God sees you and His heart is for you. He wants to make *your* dreams come true because He placed them in your heart. I've said it before, but it is worth repeating: God has a unique purpose and plan for you.

Whether you have never read the Bible through before, or whether you have read it through faithfully each year, the important takeaway for me is this. God created me and you. God loves me and you. God has a plan for my life and your life. And until I can embrace and understand my identity is in Him and from Him, then I can never fully reach my destiny.

In summary, God created us because He wants to hang out with us. He makes that clear all throughout the Bible. We are His creation and He loves us. He knew we would be better off if we didn't even know about evil. However, Adam and Eve's choice changed everything. God waited patiently for 1500 years to restore that relationship, but mankind did not respond well. Evil was in control of mankind, so He had to go back to the drawing board and start all over again.

After about 500 years He tried to establish His Kingdom by selecting and working with the Israelites. This time God made sure they knew exactly what to do so they could be prosperous and be the people that He could use to demonstrate to the world what His Kingdom looks like and draw all mankind to Him. However, that "rule and command" approach didn't work either. After another 1500 years of trying and trying to make it work, finally it was over.

But God didn't give up. He still loves us so much that He decided to send His Son Jesus Christ to earth to pay the price for all sin. By doing this, it provided a way for all of us to step into His Kingdom. The key to enter is to believe in your heart in Jesus Christ and to make Him Lord of your life.

God only wants good things for us, even when we turn away from Him. He wants to help us avoid the potholes of life. But remember, His true love for us is proven in that He gives us a choice. Just as He gave a choice to Adam and Eve back in the Garden, He gives us a choice today. He has been waiting patiently now for over 2000 years.

I don't know how much longer He is going to wait, but He tells us how it is going to be at the end of the story. God is going to "hang out" with His people in a new earth just like He has always wanted.

The choice is yours, but I really hope I will see you there.

THE SECRET TO MY SUCCESS

As I reflect back over the last fifty years, I can only shake my head in gratitude and amazement. There was no way this Costa Rican boy could have done any of this on his own. Anything I have accomplished goes back to a simple recipe for life. I learned to listen to His voice. I learned to trust God that He had my best interests at heart. And I learned to honor Him by giving back to Him a portion of what He had given me as a firstfruits of my labor, instead of the leftovers.

It has now been thirty years since I prayed that "dangerous" prayer. "God, I want to have my own business. Do something! I give You ten years of my life." During that time I learned that when we are willing to turn the controls over to Him, He is able to do amazing things far above what we could ask, think, dream, hope or desire.

That is why I share my story. Perhaps you have asked the same questions I did years ago, "What is my purpose in life?" "What am I supposed to do?" "Is there more to life than just this?" If that is where you find yourself today, then let me encourage you that you are in a good place, because those are the right questions to ask, especially when we are willing to ask them of the right Person.

If someone were to ask me what the secret to my success has been, I would have to say:

1. I have learned to trust that the Lord will turn everything for good, even when I feel I am not in control of a situation.

2. To get my mind out of the way and pay no attention to my own understanding.

3. I have learned the importance of expressing gratitude and thankfulness to the Lord every time I can for His blessings.

4. I have learned to honor God by giving Him the firstfruits of what He has given to me.

This is what I discovered as I began this journey to see if God was real. It has unlocked the mystery of the Bible and the stories within its pages. It has changed my life, and I hope it will change yours.

Scriptures

FOR OVERCOMING LIFE'S CHALLENGES

OVERCOMING TEMPTATION

Temptation will come. The Bible assures us that we will face it during the course of life. The key is how to handle it, and this scripture will show you how.

No temptation has overtaken you except what is common to mankind. And God is faithful; he will not let you be tempted beyond what you can bear. But when you are tempted, he will also provide a way out so that you can endure it (I Corinthians 10:13).

OVERCOMING WORRY

Then Jesus said to his disciples: "Therefore I tell you, do not worry about your life, what you will eat; or about your body, what you will wear. For life is more than food, and the body more than clothes.

"And do not set your heart on what you will eat or drink; do not worry about it. For the pagan world runs after all such things, and your Father knows that you need them. But seek his kingdom, and these things will be given to you as well" (Luke 12:22-23 and 29-31).

OVERCOMING SICKNESS

Praise the Lord, my soul; all my inmost being, praise his holy name. Praise the Lord, my soul, and forget not all his benefits—who forgives all your sins and heals all your diseases, who redeems your life from the pit and crowns you with love and compassion, who satisfies your desires with good things so that your youth is renewed like the eagle's (Psalm 103:1-5).

OVERCOMING FEAR

My son, do not let wisdom and understanding out of your sight, preserve sound judgment and discretion; they will be life for you, an ornament to grace your neck. Then you will go on your way in safety, and your foot will not stumble. When you lie down, you will not be afraid; when you lie down, your sleep will be sweet (Proverbs 3:21-24).

OVERCOMING SELF-RELIANCE

There was a great deal of pressure on me after I started my business. About that time I heard a song that was on the scripture below. Right then the Lord impressed on my heart that if I learned to trust Him as it said, then everything would be fine.

Trust in the Lord with all your heart and lean not on your own understanding; in all your ways submit to him, and he will make your paths straight (Proverbs 3:5-6).

I encourage you as you read through the Bible to write down scriptures that stand out to you and which speak a promise in accordance with your need. God is well able to meet that need as you pray His Word and speak it out of your mouth.

A Note

FROM THE AUTHOR

My business isn't mine at all. It's His. Even before I knew God, He knew me and had a plan for my life as He does for you. He planted within me a burning desire to have my own business. As I look back over my life from my education, meeting my wife, Lavonne, moving to the U.S. and each step after, it was His guiding hand moving me into the direction to fulfill that dream and destiny.

In the end, it took almost exactly ten years for my business to get started and established. Exactly the amount of time I gave God to prove Himself. And He did, abundantly above all I could ask, think, dream, hope or desire.

That same burning desire for life to count, I believe, is within all of us. We are each created with an innate desire that our life matters and that when our life is at its end that we can look back and know that we made a difference. We all want to know that our life mattered.

I believe we are eternal beings. What I mean by that is that after we live our seventy or eighty years of life here on this earth that there is more. I believe when we die, there is an eternity of life that awaits us. And the place where we will spend that eternity all stems from the choices we make now on this earth. That thought in itself causes me to take a good look at the direction and decisions I am making in life and determine if I need to make a course correction. For in the end it's not about being "a good person." It's about recognizing God as our Creator and making the course correction to live for Him.

I have found when I give God control and let Him take the wheel, the result is far more exciting and life-changing than what I could have ever imagined for myself.

If you want that kind of life, if you don't yet know Him but desire to, then He's ready and waiting for you to say, "God, I know You can do something with my life. I give it to You." Then buckle your seatbelt and watch what happens.

If you have made that decision after reading this book, or if you would like to contact me, you can e-mail me at: jospailau@gmail.com

About the Author

RUDY BLANCO

Rodolfo (Rudy) is the founder and president of Pathway Services, Inc., a company dedicated to serve government transportation agencies in the field of pavement and road asset management. His company collects and reports automated road condition data required to maximize the use of available resources and extend the useful life of these important transportation assets—our roads.

Now more than twenty years old, the company has grown to provide their services and equipment to more than half the state transportation agencies in the United States as well as other countries like China and Mexico.

He has a Bachelor's Degree in Ingenieria de Producción Industrial from the Instituto Tecnológico de Costa Rica and a Master of Science's Degree in Industrial Engineering from Oregon State University.

Rudy and his wife, Lavonne, have been married for thirty-seven years, and have seven children.

ENDNOTES

Chapter 9
[1]Matthew 14:13-21

Chapter 10
[2] Exodus 14
[3] Exodus 13:21-22
[4] Exodus 40:36
[5] Genesis 28:14-15
[6] Genesis 28:20-22
[7] *Genesis 30:43*
[8] Genesis 28:20
[9] Deuteronomy 26:1-4

Part 2 –
And BEYOND

Chapter 1 – Part 2
[10] Jeremiah 29:11-13
[11] Genesis 2:17
[12] Genesis 3:1-7
[13] Genesis 2:9

Chapter 2 – Part 2
[14] John 5:24
[15] Genesis 1:28

Chapter 4 – Part 2
[16] Genesis 4:3-5
[17] Genesis 4:23
[18] Genesis 6:5-8
[19] Genesis 3:13

Chapter 5-Part 2
[20] Genesis 6:11-12

[21] Merriam-Webster Dictionary online. http://www.merriam-webster.com/dictionary/corruption. Accessed August 11, 2016.
[22] Genesis 6:9
[23] Genesis 6:17
[24] Genesis 6:18
[25] Definition of the name Methusaleh, http://hermeneutics.stackexchange.com/questions/2537/what-is-the-significance-of-methuselahs-name. Accessed December 22, 2016.
[26] Genesis 9:11-13
[27] I Peter 3:18-20 MEV
[28] Genesis 9:5

Chapter 6 – Part 2
[29] Genesis 12:2-3
[30] Genesis 6:3
[31] Genesis 12:2-3
[32] Genesis 12:7
[33] Genesis 13:2
[34] Genesis 13:15
[35] Genesis 13:13
[36] Genesis 15:5
[37] Genesis 15:16
[38] Exodus 3:17
[39] Exodus 20:1-2
[40] Exodus 29:45
[41] Genesis 15:18
[42] Genesis 16:3-6
[43] Genesis 17:16-17
[44] Genesis 21:1
[45] Genesis 18:18
[46] Genesis 13:13
[47] Genesis 10:15-18
[48] Genesis 9:24-25
[49] Genesis 19:1-3
[50] Genesis 19:4-7
[51] Jude 7
[52] Genesis 22:2
[53] Genesis 26:3
[54] Genesis 26:24

55 Genesis 28:13
56 Joshua 21:43

Chapter 7 – Part 2
57 Genesis 15:13
58 Exodus 2:23-25
59 Genesis 15:13-14
60 Exodus 12:35
61 Exodus 13:17
62 Exodus 14:31
56 Exodus 15:25-26
57 Exodus 19:3-6
58 Exodus 19:8
59 Exodus 20:23
60 For a complete listing of the Ten Commandments go to http://www.10com-mandmentslist.com/
61 Leviticus 18:1-5
62 1 Corinthians 6:18-20
63 Leviticus 18:24-30
64 Exodus 19:3-6
65 Joshua 21:43-45

Chapter 8 – Part 2
66 Judges 2:10-15
67 Judges 2:16
68 Judges 2:17
69 Judges 2:18
70 1 Samuel 8:4-5
71 1 Samuel 8:7-9
72 1 Kings 6:12-13
73 1 Kings 10:23
74 1 Kings 4:34
75 1 Kings 4:29
76 1 Kings 11:1
77 1 Kings 11:2
78 Ibid.
79 Ibid.
80 1 Kings 11:4
81 2 Kings 17:7-20

[82] 2 Kings 17:29-31

[83] Leviticus 18:21

[84] Luke 18:6-8a

[85] Daniel 3:16-18

[86] Daniel 3:24-25

[87] Daniel 3:28

[88] Daniel 3:29

[89] Daniel 3:16-18

Chapter 9 – Part 2

[90] Merriam=Webster Dictionary. 'Transformation.' Merriam-Webster Dictionary. com. 2016. http://www.merriam-webster.com/dictionary/transform. Accessed December 26, 2016.

[91] Genesis 6::5-6

[92] Isaiah 42:6-9

[93] Jeremiah 31:31-34

[94] John 1:1-2,14

[95] John 1:11-12

[96] Matthew 5:44

[97] Matthew 5:40-42

[98] Matthew 7:12

[99] John 14:6

[100] Isaiah 53:5

[101] Colossians 2:13-15

[102] Galatians 3:29

[103] 2 Corinthians 5:17-19

[104] Revelation 3:20

[105] Luke 15:10

[106] Revelation 21:1-5

[107] Revelation 21:6-8

[108] John 14:26

[109] Luke 11:9-13

[110] Romans 8:38-39

[111] 1 Corinthians 2:14